Praise for *The Woman*

"No writer has more intricately explored what contemporary women means about us today than Jacey in *The Woman in the Story*. For anyone in the film industry — or anyone wanting to understand the inner machinations of the film industry — this book is a must."
—CELIA WALDEN, US Editor-at-Large, *Daily Telegraph*

"Just the byline makes me want to write a screenplay with women in it so I can use this book!"
—GILLIAN ANDERSON, actor / director, *The X-Files, The Fall, Hannibal*

"An engaging and inspirational read for filmmakers with female-driven projects. Remarkable ... truly encourages the writer to use the strategies and exercises that work for them and their characters, female, male, and trans. Essential reading!"
—HEIKE BACHELIER, filmmaker, *Feindberührung (Enemy Engagement), The Moo Man*

"Helen Jacey's passion for screen stories by women, about women, and for women preceded the recent buzz, and the creative insights she offers to writers and their producing partners will endure beyond it ... offers intellectual and practical inspiration, opening opportunities to make bold, exciting stories for the screen that celebrate female characters ... fresh-thinking, funny, and a pleasure."
—JO DILLON, EVP, Development and Production, Screen Queensland

"More relevant than ever. Helen Jacey's insights into female characters in movies are both thought-provoking and timely. Compulsive reading."
—JULIAN FARINO, director, *Entourage, Marvellous, The Oranges, Ballers*

"Delves deep and comes up with revelatory ideas about female characters ... profoundly original ... distills and transforms the way you see women from Scarlett O'Hara to Juno. Jacey provides an inventive and wonderfully clear guide to brining female characters to life. Brilliant ... the first book to think about screenwriting and gender — and about time too!"
—SARAH GAVRON, director, *Suffragette, Brick Lane*

"Guides writers to dig deeper into understanding how to write the feminine voice from the inside out. Ms. Jacey has created brilliant tools that will help writers to produce unforgettable characters."
—JEN GRISANTI, story / career consultant, author, and international speaker

"Helen's book has played an important role in the efforts to change the landscape of women characters in film. The new revisions prove females in film are an increasing force to be reckoned with, but that there is still work to be done. Points the way ahead ... a timely reminder to all filmmakers to create complex, dynamic, authentic, and truly representative roles for women in the 21st century."
—LOU HAMILTON, author and creator, *Brave New Girl*

The Woman In The Story

WRITING FEMALE CHARACTERS

in Trouble, in Love, and in Power

2nd Edition

HELEN JACEY

MICHAEL WIESE PRODUCTIONS

Published by Michael Wiese Productions

12400 Ventura Blvd. #1111

Studio City, CA 91604

(818) 379-8799, (818) 986-3408 (FAX)

mw@mwp.com

www.mwp.com

Cover design by Johnny Ink. www.johnnyink.com

Interior design by William Morosi

Copyediting by Ross Plotkin

Printed by McNaughton & Gunn, Michigan

Manufactured in the United States

Library of Congress Cataloging-in-Publication Data

Title: The woman in the story : writing female characters in trouble, in love, and in power / Helen Jacey.

Description: 2nd edition. | Studio City : Michael Wiese Productions, 2017. | Includes bibliographical references.

Identifiers: LCCN 2016030081 | ISBN 9781615932573

Subjects: LCSH: Motion picture authorship. | Motion picture plays--Technique. | Women in motion pictures. | Characters and characteristics in motion pictures.

Classification: LCC PN1996 .J26 2017 | DDC 808.2/3--dc23

LC record available at https://lccn.loc.gov/2016030081

Printed on Recycled Stock

Contents

Acknowledgments

This edition of the book would not have been possible without the commitment and enthusiasm of my publisher Michael Wiese, whose belief in the book has been enduring over the years. I am privileged to thank the brilliant Susan Cartsonis, eminent Hollywood producer, for her kindness in providing the foreword to this edition.

Also invaluable has been the support and understanding of Ken Lee at MWP. I would also like to thank Ross Plotkin for his hard work in editing.

I would also like to thank my agent Anthony Mestriner at Casarotto Ramsay for all his hard work over the years.

I am very grateful to the many talented writers, directors, and producers who attended my *Writing the Heroine's Story* seminar over the years in London, Santa Fe, Vienna, Oslo, Warsaw, Stockholm, Lausanne, Sydney, and Melbourne, and the creators across the world who have shared their female-driven screenplays with me in the development process. It has always been a two-way learning process.

Special thanks to the Seminar "godmothers" for their care on my travels, for their dedication to the female-character cause, and for helping me share, test, and refine my thinking, ideas, and strategies, including: Lucy Scher and Briony Hanson; Martha Coleman, Veronica Gleeson, and Jo Dillon at Screen Queensland; Jacqueline Surchat at Focal, Zurich; Oliver Dixon, Film Region Stockholm-Mälardalen and Mattias Ehrenberg, KultureKraft; Judith di Salvo Hennessy and Linda McDill, New Mexico Women in Film and TV; Siri Senje, Jan Erik Holst at the Norwegian Film Institute; Katarzyna Dlugosz; Wilbirg Brainin-Donnenberg, Screenwriters Forum, Vienna, for being the immense catalyst for special times in Vienna; Iris Zappe-Heller and Roland Teichmann, Austrian Film Institute. For hosting me at special events focusing on creating female characters: Vivid Film Festival and Screen New South Wales (thanks especially to Megan Simpson Huberman); Birds Eye View Film Festival; Cornwall Film Festival; Women in Film and Television (UK); London International Film Festival; and all the other event organizers who have hosted me. For all the administrators and technicians who provided me with indispensable support, a special thanks for their patience.

For support and efforts in spreading the word: Celia Walden, Randee Dawn, Helen Jack, Nikki Baughan, Sandra Donskyte, Elinor Burns, Gareth Wiley, Julian Farino, Sarah Gavron, Melissa Silverstein, Gillian Anderson, Suzanne Mackie, Robert Jones, Jen Grisanti, Felix Vasquez, Jr., Alexis Krasilovsky, Jonathan Sothcott, Tim John, Dave Watson, Lou Hamilton, Sue Brooks, Alison Tilson, Heike Bachelier, Sandra Cain, Kelly Marshall, Kate Leys, Patti McCarthy, Elizabeth English, Linda Seger, Kate Kinninmont, Posy Brewer, Rebecca Brand, Kate Machi, Jane Kirkham, Craig Batty, Mary Evans, Jule Selbo, Jill Nelmes, Heather Savigny, Claire Jenkins, and everyone else who has helped in some way, which I truly appreciate.

Last but by no means least, all those across the world who have simply read the book and gotten in touch to share their characters and their stories.

To Patrick

Foreword

*T*he updated second edition of *The Woman in the Story* is timely and welcome. Since the first edition of this wonderfully intelligent book in 2010, awareness of gender inequity in media both behind and in front of the camera has reached critical mass.

The news media regularly documents actresses like Jennifer Lawrence, Patricia Arquette, and Cate Blanchett, who speak out about inequity in wages and opportunity. Male actors and producers like Bradley Cooper and Judd Apatow are standing with them. Writers and directors, both male and female, are ready to explore the fullness of what a woman can or should be through the way that they work and the stories that they tell. But the roles and the writing must be there to meet the talent and the financiers who recognize that the feminine perspective must be represented. Helen Jacey's important book lights the way for artists. It's a book for those in the film and television business who care about the female audience, and people who love screen stories and want to understand what makes the great ones work.

I'm a film producer and it pains me that for too long Hollywood and the international filmmaking community have missed the point that we leave money on the table when we don't make films for and about women. As an industry, we miss the opportunity to illuminate, inspire, and entertain audiences internationally by neglecting to tell specific, dimensional, and ultimately fascinating stories of the female half of the human race in favor of predominantly male protagonists. Helen Jacey tells us why and how to tell those stories well. And when we tell those stories well, everyone wins.

Numerous studies, including yearly ones published by the MPAA, reveal that women aren't just equal consumers of film and television, they often outnumber men at the box office. Marketers have long known that women lead the general audience to what they should and will watch. Boys and young men continue to drift away from film and television and toward gaming, while women of all ages continue to be loyal and avid consumers of screen stories. The size and influence of the audience for female protagonists demands that the women portrayed on the screen, whatever size screen, inhabit interesting stories and play dimensional roles, roles that are original and universal. *The Woman in the Story* shows us how to accomplish this by challenging us to think and rethink what we know about making truly great characters and stories.

As I read the book, I couldn't help but get excited about new possibilities for characters in films I'm developing, and even about one film I begin shooting this month. *The Woman in the Story* not only guided me to expand my thinking about female characters I'm developing; it stimulated me to think of new stories to develop about the female experience. It literally expanded my thinking and my mind.

Helen Jacey's ideas about gender in screen storytelling are also a perfect antidote to the notion that in order to even the gender playing field, one only needs to flip male characters by "putting them in a skirt" to make a female character. Men and women are not the same, and Jacey recognizes differences sensitively and intelligently, embracing them with great knowledge and deep understanding. Certainly recent film hits like *The Hunger Games*, *Maleficent*, *Twilight*, *Frozen*, and *Trainwreck*, and television shows like *Transparent*, *Orphan Black*, *Orange Is the New Black*, and *Girls* portray the unique experiences of the feminine journey. *The Woman in the Story* guides us to original, true, and honest storytelling by challenging old ideas in a way that will help writers and those who love good and dimensional writing to think about the female psyche in dramatic literature in a new and fresh way.

Jacey smartly challenges conventional wisdom about writing for women. Lately the film industry has decided that the conventional wisdom is that the "romantic comedy is dead." It turns out that conventional wisdom in screenwriting, and in life, really isn't wisdom at all. In the world of Jacey's book, the romantic comedy is redefined each time it's written. It's no longer a rehash of what once worked; it's guided by the challenges that a unique character faces. If the lead character is unattractive in her behavior or appearance, will the audience find her unforgivable and unappealing? Can she no longer be a protagonist? If the plot doesn't fit neatly into a genre description, does that make it any less authentic? In this great book, Jacey shows us how to find the interesting corners of character and story, and celebrate them to make something fresh, new, and true.

I hope you enjoy the book as much as I did.

Susan Cartsonis
Producer (*Deidra & Laney Rob a Train*, *Carrie Pilby*, *The DUFF*, *Where the Heart Is*, *What Women Want*)

Introduction
to the Second Edition

*I*f *The Woman in the Story* is anything, it's a set of suggestions, one writer to another, during those highs and lows that come part and parcel with developing a screenplay. Maybe you just need to step outside your story for a while and look at it from another vantage point. Maybe you need a little extra nourishment for the more creatively barren times, or something to help smooth over the rougher moments of development hell. Finding a character and bringing her to life plunges us deep into many parallel processes: thinking, processing, mulling, being illuminated, being blocked, and being re-inspired, not to mention finding time for real life in between.

Creating a character's identity and life is an awesome process. All of a sudden, we are in a relationship with this character as a parent, a god, a friend, and an ally. We are protective and possessive, thinking that as writers, we know them better than anyone else does! Of course we do; we invented them. But similar to our relationships in life, character development requires us to co-parent, to trust in others, to take others' advice, and ultimately to let go. More often than not, our characters have a say in who they are because they have formed a bizarre allegiance with our creative unconscious and together have come up with a very different take on who and what they want to be. Many writers can relate to the uncanny moment when their characters seem to behave or speak in ways their creators didn't intend!

Ideally, this book is aimed at every writer who is juggling and multitasking the nurture and growth of his or her characters to the point of letting go. Wherever you are on your journey, whether you are a seasoned pro or a student writer, the book is a resource for *your* creative path.

Gender Baggage

This book offers a pure and simple focus on thinking about female protagonists and the ways in which the gender of your character can and might impact your writing. "Can" because, like it or not, gender issues can creep in when we least expect them; it's the world we live in. "Might" because you, the writer, might have a specific intention to create certain kinds of female characters who reflect something you want to say about the world we live in *or* the world your character lives in, and how that world affects girls, boys, men, women, non-binary individuals, robots, mythical creatures, and any other being.

All these "cans" and the "mights" affecting or influencing your choices for your story with a female protagonist could be called the "gender baggage" that we often pick up and carry along the road of development. This book aims to lessen the load.

A Little Herstory

The book came out almost a century after the first how-to on writing female characters. The problems facing the female character on screen were even rife in the days of vamps, vixens, and spunky gals who strutted their stuff in front of the earliest rolling spools. Lizzie Francke's fascinating book *Script Girls* led me to the existence of Elinor Glyn, a novelist turned

Hollywood "photoplay" writer, who in 1922 published her book *The Elinor Glyn System of Writing*, which described what heroines should and shouldn't do and be, guidelines that seem very old-fashioned by contemporary standards. Almost a century later, in spite of the vote and various waves of feminism and post-feminism, we still agonize over female characters and take our time getting female characters to their rightful place on screen. We must continue — it took over one hundred years to make a major motion picture about suffragettes!

On publication in 2010, the first edition of this book met with such a hungry and enthusiastic reception from so many writers and filmmakers all over the world — both women and men — it was clear that the book had hit a proverbial nail on the head. I was thrilled that the book clearly filled a gap in screenwriting guides, succeeding because of its simple mission to help writers create strong, memorable female characters and have some creative, thought-provoking fun in the process. It has been frequently hailed as the go-to resource for helping writers think about their female character and come to grips with common issues and concerns that female protagonism presents. Many people said it was useful for developing female *and* male characters, which is fantastic.

Ripples to Sea Changes

Like all surprising characters, the book led me on a heroine's journey that was surprising, urgent, meandering, inclusive, passionate, wide ranging, emotional, hilarious, and illuminating. The book took me to many places where the cause of the female character was debated, discussed, and developed. Discussions often ranged far from the book's core focus on developing the female protagonist. The obstacles writers face, the perennial inequality of the roles and opportunities offered women creatives, and the lack of onscreen female characters that reflect the true diversity of women's lives are all concerns connected to the book's stated purpose of helping writers develop memorable female protagonists. It is, after all, the female protagonist who is the ultimate creative embodiment of so many processes — creative and industrial — that the writer has experienced and negotiated. The groundbreaking work of innumerable institutions and organizations — including Women in Film, the Geena Davis Institute, Miss Represen-tation, WomenandHollywood.com, the Athena Film Festival, Birds Eye View, the Underwire Festival, the Everyday Sexism blog, and countless more big and small groups — testify to this. The female protagonist in all her nebulous yet sometimes fragile glory is like a mothership of debates. Research from the Center for the Study of Women in Television & Film, University of San Diego, The Media, Diversity, & Social Change Initiative, USC's Annenberg School for Communication and Journalism, and the Geena Davis Institute tells us that female writers and female characters remain outnumbered in terms of produc-tions, and female-led teams create different representations of female characters that are less stereotypical. If you want to review the research findings and statistics available about diver-sity issues affecting female characters and stories, the annual reports these institutions compile reveal the real lowdown.

Bigger, Bolder, and Better

Since the book's first publication, new female characters have broken through and ventured forth into uncharted story terri-tory. Katniss Everdeen in *The Hunger Games*; Alicia Florrick in *The Good Wife* (not forgetting Kalinda, Diane, Lucca, and Elspeth); Piper Chapman and all the inmates in *Orange Is the New Black*; Merida in *Brave*; and Joy and Sadness in *Inside Out*, to name a few. Black and ethnically diverse characters lead series and films, such as Olivia Pope in *Scandal* and Annalise Keating in *How to Get Away With Murder*.

If you want to see a show or movie with memorable female characters, you don't have to look very far. Internationally, *Suffragette*, *Eye in the Sky*, *Mustang*, *Phoenix*, *Wadjda*, *The Babadook*, and *The Dressmaker* are among the multitude of wonderful films from across the world that make us sit up and notice as they reveal new perspectives on and possibilities for female characters. Over the past five years, we have lived through a pervasive feminist revolution in storytelling, and it isn't going away. Neither are complicated, diverse, fascinating, and memorable female characters — and more are reaching the screens every day. Perhaps these female protagonists exist on screen now often because they, or their creator, just didn't have a chance before. They fill gaps, they entertain in new ways, they give a female point of view, they dismantle stereotypes that are overly familiar and clichéd, and they generate new types and roles that have fewer restrictions and push more boundaries.

We are also living in an age where transgender and non-binary characters are starting to appear on screen, those characters who have to negotiate their lives and loves in what can still be a very rigidly defined or hostile world. Whether we choose our gender or stick with the one assigned to us, an ideal world is a truly equal world where everyone's human rights, including the right to identify however one wants, are honored and respected — a world where gender causes no division or exploitation. In film and TV, sci-fi and fantasy genres often give more scope for writers to create equal worlds. It is the real world, past or present, which can present writers with more challenges around gender and how it influences female characterization. Are you a utopian-minded writer, or do the darkest and most depraved worlds seem better suited to your storytelling? Perhaps you like characters who lead relatively empowered lives? Wherever you are on the spectrum, it will influence your approach to female character-building and your themes.

Creative Tensions

Evocatively expressing one's feelings about gender can be the broadest of dilemmas a writer faces when s/he chooses a female protagonist. The writer will often reflect on the gender baggage both they and their female protagonists could be lugging around. Even with the increased focus on female characters, creative anxiety persists. Many writers who have read this book or attended my *Writing the Heroine's Story* seminar share similar dilemmas and questions:

- *I like her, but my producer/director/friend thinks she's unlikable and wants me to change her...*
- *How can I avoid stereotypes?*
- *I just want to learn some ways of making her really interesting and know I'm doing that well*
- *How can I make her believable yet have a seemingly impossible goal (for a woman)?*
- *How is my character's gender affecting my choices? How can I become conscious of these?*
- *What's the difference between the hero's and heroine's journeys?*
- *I don't feel others identify with my female character. Help!*
- *What tools could I use to offload the "gender baggage" that female characters seem to lug around?*
- *How can I make her strong yet appealing to those with conventional ideas about femininity?*

Anxieties are usually very personal to the writer, because our female characters are our inventions, and a bit like proud parents, we worry if we are doing the right thing by them. Do these concerns risk us abandoning our character before she finds her feet? As a writer, you may feel uncomfortable about certain aspects of a female character's identity, choices, traits, and behaviors, and anxious about how they will be received when you show them to others. Is she too provocative? Too violent? Too selfish? Too old? Too ugly? Your character may feel slightly weighed down by gender baggage in numerous other ways due to the roles she assumes in her world, or expectations in your own culture about what is permissible or acceptable for you to write about. Whatever the sex of the character, as writers, we can't escape dipping into a mixed bag of gender stereotypes, acceptable clichés, and/or completely original aspects of character. How you work with these will ultimately shape how dimensional and unique your character becomes to you.

It's clear that choosing a female character to lead the story produces many questions for writers in development — and in my experience, far more than writing a male character seems to. Are there just some kinds of story that a male hero more easily fits? Are male characters still being sent on bigger and better adventures, having more fun generally, or are they more resistant to change because the audience doesn't mind masculine stereotypes? Male protagonists can be as loaded with gender baggage as their female counterparts anyway. Overly familiar stereotypes still push through every year — "loner cop," "tough guy," "heroic dad," "downtrodden nerd who needs to man up"; these can be as problematic for writers and audiences as female stereotypes. The voices complaining about the stereotyping of men, the lack of male vulnerability on screen, and the female objectification of men are far less clamorous, however.

While the focus on diversity on screen is increasing, there are still steep mountains to cross, cliff edges and dead ends for characters of both sexes. There are still many things female characters haven't been or done on screen *as the protagonist*. These might very well already exist in the imaginations of writers who can't yet travel the distance; they still don't fit or resonate with industry stakeholders due to their characters' identity, age, sexuality, ability, ethnic group, orientation, outrageous personality, or shocking choices. One thing is certain: the female protagonist is still emerging, and she will remain so as women's lives, experiences, and roles remain in flux.

This edition goes into more depth about the Heroine's Journey, linking it an approach using *Phases* as a way of building your female protagonist's emotional identity to propel her story. The expanded exploration of types and Role-Choices will inform some of your "gender-mindful" creative decisions, as well as stir your imagination, for both your female and male characters may wish to subvert gender as their stories progress. The edition has some new case studies, from film and TV, with female characters who appeared in the last five years and who broke new ground in unique and memorable ways. The only basis for selection is that they easily illustrate a creative model or have a standout quality that is useful to explore. If the characters you have loved don't appear, then you can always consider the book's creative models in context to your favorite characters. Do bear in mind that as popular TV series can run for years, female protagonists' plots and characters might have radically changed since the time this book was published.

Over to You

The approaches herein may enable you to explore a wide range of creative paradigms, to trigger ideas, and to push yourself further and deeper into your character and story world with a focus on what it means for *you*, the writer or developer, to have a female character. If there is any rule of thumb, do what feels good rather than what feels right!

CHAPTER 1

The Power of the Female Protagonist

*B*efore we get started, sit back and think long and hard about why you want to choose a female protagonist in the first place. Hopefully, at the most basic level you want to further the cause of womanhood with your story, and obviously you want a female point of view.

Some of your reasons might echo any of these motivations:

- *It's a biopic about a famous woman's life*
- *It's a true story about a little-known woman*
- *To show a woman getting over betrayal/trauma and finding a new life*
- *It's an older woman/younger man love story*
- *She's a badass hit-woman loner*
- *It's about a woman finding out what she really wants out of love and life*
- *It's a rite of passage as a girl becomes a woman*
- *She's the first black woman president*

- *Her son is kidnapped, her divorced husband still loves her, and she fights the baddies to make sure her son gets home safe*
- *She has no love interest whatsoever*
- *It's about a group of nuns in a convent in 18th-century Spain*
- *It's about a group of nuns who run an international drug cartel*
- *To show the struggles of female artists*
- *My heroine's a survivor against all odds*
- *I want her to be strong without giving up her femininity*
- *It's a romcom about undateables!*
- *It's about a group of female friends who set up a commune*
- *To show the intensity of a lesbian relationship*
- *It's about an older woman who wants to be a man, but is it too late?*
- *She's a female android who...*
- *It's a fantasy about a matriarchal society*
- *I want to write a thriller/drama/horror with a main character who just happens to be a woman*

Do any of these feel familiar? If so, it is no surprise; they are all motivated by a unifying creative urge — to explore a female character coping with a situation and how her gender has relevance. The last bullet point above is often uttered by writers who feel the sex and gender of their character make no difference to the story; they are writing about human beings, who in their mind are essentially all the same and are all equal.

It could be useful to summarize some of the factors behind choosing a female protagonist like this:

- To portray **the issues** that affect women's lives

- To create a **strongly emotional story**

- To **celebrate a real woman**'s achievement or wonderful personality

- To **reject conventional femininity** — to create female characters who show us ways of being (for females) that aren't limited by typical and familiar roles or expectations of women

- To **subvert conventional femininity** — to defy and play around with stereotypes, norms, clichés, and ideals of females

- To show "**gender neutrality**" — to treat all your characters exactly the same. None of your characters have any different experiences or attitudes because of their sex

Likewise, choosing a male protagonist might be defined by a different set of motivations:

- To show **bigger and better** outer quests, sometimes where **violence and action** dominate

- To have **fewer issues about being single** or childless/unmarried/sexaholic/unattractive if they are of a certain age

- To avoid **a focus on love and relationships**

- To show **older characters doing interesting things**

- To glorify and celebrate **bad behavior or morally reprehensible choices** as triumphant ways of being

It's not often that writers say, "to explore a man in a woman's world," or "to reject the shackles of masculine roles that trap and define him" (although writers of male-to-female trans characters might).

At this point, you might be thinking: *What? This is way too complicated! I'm just telling a story!* You're right; it's complicated! The good news is that complicated doesn't mean hard work. Creating characters is fun, stimulating, and challenging. Yes, complicated can be complex, but the more complex you find the process, the more layered your character could end up. She will reflect your complex thinking, somehow. Hard work seldom goes to waste, but you can assure it won't if you use creativity, particularly when working on the nebulous concepts of gender and character. The bad news is that... well, there is no bad news, if you're prepared to be honest about your preconceptions and underlying attitudes, and open your eyes to new ways of thinking.

Being WISE (Writer's Ideological Slant Effect)

Every dramatic and creative step you take in developing your character will be shaped by your attitudes, values, and beliefs about her gender. Just as females and males are assigned feminine and masculine gender roles at birth, you control the depth and nature of the gender role you assign your female (and male) characters. Whomever she is, and wherever she is from, your female protagonist will likely have a gendered identity. And as it goes for most real cultures, expectations placed on the female sex are still bound up with values and attitudes about femininity. Subtle and not-so-subtle nuances creep in: the forty- or fiftysomething female protagonist who is single, and who doesn't have kids, has a few issues about this, and they creep into the story. Or she is sixty plus, and her story is immersed in family or surrogate-family issues. We have a tendency to give the stories we write a gendered slant that often reflects what we feel to be acceptable or true.

This "slant effect" is most obvious in the way you have constructed the identity of your main character. It can also be detected in the journey your character follows, the story structure, the secondary and tertiary characters, the use of conflict and union, the tone, the style, and the way you've handled genre in your screenplay. Gender is a bit like dye that's run from the main article (your character) in your wash (all the other story elements). It colors everything, but not in a uniform way. There are always some surprises revealed by the color-change process! Essentially, being WISE is a way of getting in touch with some of your innermost thoughts about gender, and how they play out in your writing. How WISE you want to be (or not) is entirely up to you! But it might help you find out what some of your deeper motivations are, and your own particular slant effect. What is your story with a female character going to say about women and their feminine roles?

If you write with a lot of female main characters, you will soon see certain ideas and themes re-emerging in each project. Sometimes, even if you've chosen a distinctly different protagonist, as well as a different "story world," plot, theme, and even genre, you know you are covering old ground. It's as if a certain *sensibility* or an *ideological slant* is infusing your work when it comes to the female protagonist and the story she's telling. If you haven't been writing for long, then this feeling is similar to when you have a familiar reaction to movies or shows with female leads. Some might profoundly move you, resonating deeply. Others might leave you feeling angry and dissatisfied with the character, her choices, or the moral implications of the story. Some might actively repulse you! There's something about how the protagonist reinforces or antagonizes your worldview. These instinctive and creative responses could boil down to the human need in writers to see a true reflection of our core beliefs, which have been created by our personal experience and understanding of life and which play out in our writing.

I call this effect the Writer's Ideological Slant Effect (WISE for short). Your WISE is unique to you as a writer; it is part of your voice, and what makes your writing distinctive. Your unique character and story can reveal tones and shades about your own personal "take" on masculinity and femininity — attitudes and values from your own identity, your own lived experience, you own way of seeing the world. Nobody has lived your life, had your life experiences, shares your emotional makeup, possesses your DNA. This world will reflect what you want to say about femininity whether you are saying it consciously or unconsciously. You, as originating creator, will define your character, her choices, and her journey according to these factors, whether you are fully aware of them or not. You are WISE whether you like it or not!

The Feminine SuperThemes

The Feminine SuperThemes is a creative model that can help you explore your way of being WISE through choices you have made about your female character's gendered identity, i.e., how she identifies with ways of being when it comes to gender. The model is a typological one, which means it's a system of categorizing femininity through types, but it loosely draws on the observations of thousands of female characters, and almost as many conversations with writers! The SuperThemes can be seen as resonant with your underlying core values and beliefs behind your choice of a female character, and the ones you aspire to share with your audience through story.

A Feminine SuperTheme reflects your worldview and subconscious attitudes about gender through your female protagonist's identification with gender expectations and norms in her world.

Think of a Feminine SuperTheme as if you are wearing tinted shades when you write your female-led story. You see your character and her attitude, and experience her "feminine" identity world through a gendered hue. She could be a stay-at-home mom or a radical feminist. As her creator, her identity and worldview, and ultimately what she learns and how she changes, will be pretty strong indicators of your own values. The goals and obstacles you give her will be shaped by her identity and value system, and driven by your own way of being WISE, your ideological slant.

Your story might have several SuperThemes permeating throughout the character's experience and identity, often layered together.

The Feminine SuperThemes are:

- **Familiar** Femininity
- **Feel-Good** Femininity
- **Fighting** Femininity
- **Fantasy** Femininity
- **Fecund** Femininity
- **Future** Femininity
- **Felonious** Femininity

FEMININE SUPERTHEME 1:
Familiar Femininity

The Familiar Femininity character and her journey are exactly that: resoundingly familiar to us. She reflects what most of the audience would connect with as a pretty believable version of a female character's real-life experiences. She exhibits strongly relatable values and attitudes in which her emotional well-being and those she cares about are central. Thrown off course, she will do her best to sort herself out eventually by facing up to her struggles. When the Familiar Femininity character encounters the dark side of life, she may be in trouble unless the situation enables her to examine who she is, and change. She aspires to be a functioning human being even if she starts out or ends up an outsider. She wants to belong, to make connections and attain stability, even if she goes about this the wrong way or if aspects of her personality don't help. She might identify with conventional expectations of a mother, a wife, and a professional; multitasking and "having it all" all too often present her with dilemmas. If her life was perfect, she would do her best to be caring, nurturing, and non-abandoning to those she loves.

Close relationships are very important to the Familiar Femininity character because they feature so heavily in her life; if she hasn't got them, she tends to need them. Significant others might be her biggest headache, but they can also be her anchor and her emotional touchstone. Her work and life outside close relationships can also cause conflict, or put her in jeopardy. If this threatens her significant others in some way, it will be up to her to resolve these.

By and large, this character pretty much accepts society's norms, and lives within them. She may gripe about unfairness, but there isn't a supremely feminist agenda driving her lifestyle choices. Rocking the boat is not her style, but she needs to be true to herself and her values for as far and as long as she can — or have these values tested. She wants or needs to live her life authentically, or else work out what being true to herself actually is.

Internal conflicts tend to revolve around low self-esteem, guilt, inadequacy, fear, shame, loss of identity, and other forms of deeply personal emotional pain. External conflicts tend to be those inflicted by significant others — parents, partners, lovers, children, colleagues, or work and community figures — whose actions trigger change and growth. Since the Familiar Femininity character doesn't make it her life's mission to challenge oppression in her life, she doesn't generally have a problem with men as a sex, or with the masculine gender, but rather with individuals. When she encounters a challenge stemming from sexual discrimination and becomes motivated to do something about it, then her identity (and the story) can get more radical; this is when the Familiar SuperTheme gets a hue of Fighting Femininity (see below). However bad life gets, she frequently ends up with her core value system firmly intact, if a little shaken.

As a writer who depicts Familiar Femininity:

- You might say, *"I'm not out to change the world with my character; I'm just saying it how it is."*

- Fundamentally, you want your character to be relatable.

- You know the importance of self-esteem and support systems for healthy and positive ways of living, but are also aware how difficult most people find sustaining these systems to be.

- You have a strong motivation to create a female character who you feel is grounded in "here and now" reality and feels contemporary.

- You want to tell a good story that celebrates everyday women in their ordinary lives.

- You have a strong affection for genuine and "real" women who have to face complicated and challenging situations.

- You may take her on big emotional journeys where her life changes because she changes.

- In terms of feminism, you accept that some things are equal for women, some things aren't, and you aren't afraid to show and explore both sides. But identifying as a feminist would be going too far; you're more of a "humanist" and believe we all have problems, whoever we are. You don't have issues with either sex.

- Your character tends to be consumed by making changes on the personal level. You enjoy immersing yourself in emotional stories with a heart of gold, even if the gold is a little tarnished in places.

FAMILIAR FEMININITY CHARACTER STUDY:
Alicia Florrick in *The Good Wife*

The hugely popular series *The Good Wife* features fortysomething Alicia Florrick, who returns to practice law at one of Chicago's leading firms after raising her kids and being a housewife. The series provides an almost iconic representation of the Familiar Femininity SuperTheme — at least in its first few seasons. The show is a great example of the slow, meandering arcs that are offered by long-running series, and that enable writing teams to follow a character as she grows and develops. Alicia starts out as a woman returner, someone who needs to become the provider to her kids after husband Peter Florrick is sentenced to jail, having been found guilty of corruption as District Attorney. The cases of the week in the early seasons are handled by Alicia using intuition, compassion, and empathy toward her clients, directly borne out of her own experience as an outsider.

Primarily identifying as a wife and mother, Alicia has a vertical learning curve to adapt and survive in her profession. She is mentored by Diane, the feminist CEO, who has not had kids and puts work first. Initially, Alicia wants to above all be a good mom who genuinely does her best for her kids, Grace and Zach. The job has to come second. Alicia is loyal and hardworking, with strong moral values. She stands by her man for the good of the family, despite his extreme betrayal of sleeping with hookers. This utter rejection of her core values by Peter provides the biggest external and internal conflict to Alicia: How can she adjust to life, and find happiness and self-esteem again? How can she remain a good wife even though she is married to somebody who doesn't share her moral values regarding marriage? Alicia's hurt and anger is not expressed by rage, revenge, demand for an instant divorce, or punitively denying Peter the right to see his kids. She's a stayer. As something of an introvert, Alicia retreats inwardly, finding it hard to reach out to others while her wounds slowly heal. She resists an affair with Will Gardner for as long as she can. Her nickname, given by characters who've come up against Alicia's rock-solid core values, is "St. Alicia."

As the seasons progress, continuing to play her part as the supportive wife to aid Peter's rehabilitation as a political player becomes increasingly fraught for Alicia; it begins to feels empty and hypocritical. She succumbs to her desire for Will, and they have a secret affair. The clandestine and seedy side of life is fundamentally opposed to Alicia's moral values, and she gives Will an ultimatum: commit openly, and face the consequences for family, work, and reputation, or she will end it. Will wants Alicia, but Peter's political strategist Eli Gold sabotages the affair.

Hurt by Will's seeming lack of interest, Alicia throws herself into her career and continues to publicly fulfill her role as a good wife. But Will's death, Peter's constant affairs, Alicia's foiled attempt at becoming District Attorney, and the loss of her law firm leave Alicia once again questioning her identity and the meaning of her life — she's grieving and broke, publicly humiliated and professionally sabotaged. Alicia has to rebuild her life yet again, finding meaning and finding herself. Acting the good wife in public finally becomes intolerable to Alicia, increasingly allergic to being played. She suffers a breakdown, and finally lets someone else in on an emotional level — a young woman, Lucca Quinn. Over the course of her long journey, Alicia's worldview develops tinges of Fighting Femininity, although she's never an out-and-out feminist. Alicia finally chooses her own identity beyond marriage, beyond self-restraint, beyond always doing and being the right thing for others to live on her terms. The very good wife finally wises up and demands a divorce.

Other examples of Familiar Femininity are:

Philomena: Philomena, an elderly woman, wants to find the baby she once gave up to an orphanage run by nuns. With the help of a journalist, she travels back to the orphanage to find out information about him, only to discover that her son died in adulthood, and that the nuns had actively prevented their reconnection. Philomena stays true to her values of compassion and forgiveness while experiencing the deepest pain.

The Durrells: Louisa is the mother of four teenagers living in the gloomy 1930s seaside town of Bournemouth, England. She is finding it hard to cope since the death of her husband, hitting the gin every night. On a whim she cashes out and uproots her children to Corfu in the hope of a better life. Resettling is stressful, but with the help of friendly Greeks and the beauty of the island, Louisa achieves her dream of making her children happy.

FEMININE SUPERTHEME 2:
Feel-Good Femininity

Feel-Good Femininity is the driving motivation behind films with female characters who want to live life on their terms — which often includes self-expression, freedom, hedonism, and autonomy — and are managing to do it just fine, without needing to "aggressively" take on the system. Conflicts for this type of character are largely internal. She's nobody's victim but her own, and however bad other people get, they can do worse than inflaming her dysfunction. If your character has got issues with men, she will engage in the battle of the sexes with zeal, but will be learning her own lessons about herself and her life along the way. Male characters in these stories are never out-and-out bad guys, oppressing the female lead or destroying her sense of identity. If they are negative or hostile, they reflect her own inner problems, the state in which she might be emotionally stuck. The Feel-Good character might have emotional wounds, but she will heal them in order to find the right soulmate or be happily single. She can be described as *postfeminist* as she embraces a distinct "having it all" mentality without too much strife; she just takes her freedom and pursuit of life on her terms for granted. She will laugh at what's great and what sucks about being a woman in equal measure. Her emotional arc tends to result in an upbeat and conventional happy ending, reflecting the human desire to feel understood, to belong, and to find that special person who truly gets her. Life should be fulfilling, joyous, romantic, sexual, and positive. Above all, it should feel good!

The widespread appeal of these films and shows for women is based on their celebration of female empowerment and a "feel good" sensibility. Tonally they are light, and may be comedic or dramedic. They appeal to our emotions in a light and carefree way, enabling us to escape rather than confront. These films take their rightful place alongside comfort food and shopping binges.

As a writer who depicts Feel-Good Femininity:

- You don't like to write anything too heavy or too dark. You're writing for audiences who want entertainment that makes them feel emotionally upbeat.

- You don't want to put your heroine in extreme jeopardy; you want your character to be protected from the stark reality of poverty, ill health, inequality, racism, sexism, etc.

- You believe we are free to make choices and live with the consequences, or at least learn from mistakes in a positive and life-affirming way, and so does your character.

- You believe love and romance are important for happiness, and they can make life better, even when the chips are down.

- You like the fact that women are able to redefine femininity for themselves in every area of their lives: sex, romance, relationships, work.

- You believe a character can turn her life around through self-growth.

- You are probably deeply fascinated by the emotional journeys of empowered female characters who love and deserve to "have it all" in today's world — lovers, kids, jobs, beauty, fun, friends...

- You can relate to some postfeminist ideals: having it all and achieving superwoman-like aptitudes.

Ricki can barely pay her bills, her day job in a supermarket is dull and demeaning, and her apartment is a dump, but she's not tormented by her situation in life. Why? Because Ricki once did what most people spend their lives avoiding: she gave up everything — her young kids, her husband, her security — to pursue her dream of being a rock star. The dream didn't bring her fame and fortune, but that wasn't why she did it; music is her gift and the love of her life. Her creative force and love of music is central to her identity. Hitting sixty or thereabouts, Ricki is still managing to do what she loves, performing rock music in a local bar and giving pleasure to her fans. She dresses how she wants, she has a hot boyfriend (her bass guitarist), and the regulars love her music. She's a true rock chick, to the core. Ricki's deepest inner conflict is a fear of commitment, since it might curtail her freedom; she knows what she can and can't tolerate. She keeps her devoted boyfriend at arm's length without any great soul searching or guilt. Having walked out on her marriage and three kids when they were little, because life as a mother and wife just wasn't an option for her, Ricki is now estranged from her family. When her daughter is dumped by her fiancé and has a breakdown, Ricki's wealthy and remarried ex-husband summons her to support their daughter.

After some hesitation, Ricki finally visits her family, who are now based in a sterile gated community for the wealthy. Ricki does the right thing, but it costs her by being pushed out of her comfort zone and being forced to witness her children's emotional scars. Staying true to herself, she takes her adult children's mixed and somewhat infantile emotions toward her with dignity and good grace. She shows she is there for them, in her free-spirited way, without compromising who she is or changing for them. She won't be manipulated into saying she's sorry. Ricki identifies with Familiar Femininity as she rediscovers new relationships with her children and tries her best to help them work on their issues. She has a Fighting Femininity moment onstage in the pub when she angrily lets rip that because she's a woman and rocker, she experiences a sexual double standard, citing Mick Jagger's many children by different women and the lack of public outcry it inspires. In fact, he's revered. Eventually, Ricki proves her enduring love to her children by giving them the only thing she has to offer by playing a song at her son's wedding. She shows gratitude to her husband's second wife, who raised her kids. Ricki's children learn that a mother who leaves to be true to herself and whose ambitions take her outside the family can still be a human being who loves them dearly.

Other examples of Feel-Good Femininity are:

Trainwreck: Sexually liberated and commitment-phobic Amy learns that Father — who has raised her to believe that humans weren't meant for monogamy — doesn't always know best. Amy has no positive internal role models to draw upon when she falls in love with a highly functional sports doctor. She learns that to earn his trust and have a healthy relationship, she has to unlearn a lot of negative behavior patterns.

Girls: Hannah, Marnie, Jessa, and Shoshanna try to work out who they are and what they want as young women in vibrant and artistic contemporary New York.

FEMININE SUPERTHEME 3:
Fighting Femininity

Fighting Femininity is exactly how it sounds: the female character is driven to action to confront the worst sides of sexism, inequality, and the cruelty of "The Patriarchy." Patriarchy describes the system that a Fighting Femininity female character meets head-on because her core values do not allow her, or others, to be constrained or subjected to a sexual double standard, one that benefits men and those who conform to or uphold the system. Even in the domestic scenario, the Fighting Femininity female character will break out of oppressive circumstances and relationships to find a life free from the control of others. Male characters in Fighting Femininity shows and films can reflect sexism and misogyny benignly or as instruments of the regime. They can be cruel control freaks or powerless good guys. Sometimes they are equal partners, giving solidarity to the female character in her quest for freedom or justice. Female characters that uphold the system can be reprehensible to the Fighting Femininity female protagonist. Conflict in Fighting Femininity stories tends to be external, deeply layered, and dark. The obstacles to freedom are huge and challenging. Internal conflict is commonly experienced by the protagonist in terms of inadequacy and divided loyalties. If she is true to her beliefs, how would those dearest to her suffer? Consider the abused wife who wants to leave home, but her culture/friends/family would disapprove. Many films with female protagonists from world cinema reflect Fighting Femininity, reminding the audience that many women's lives in different parts of the world remain unequal and oppressive.

As a writer who depicts Fighting Femininity:

- You create characters who, despite being victimized and with little chance of living life on their own terms, find it within themselves to get up and fight.

- You love writing "women against the system" journeys, even if the main character doesn't win. Bleak endings make you all the more determined to show the world how corrupt and unequal things are.

- You're a champion of the underdog.

- You like writing about female characters who take on the boys' club, push through the glass ceiling, and rather than lean in, do all they can to get the hell out.

- You're strongly motivated to explore the masculine power structures that have curtailed women's lives for millennia, and you are motivated to write a story to prove it's still going on.

- You want a strong female protagonist who has genuine solidarity with other females (and supportive males) who threaten "The Patriarchy."

- You are irked by seeing female characters on screen that reflect overt and hidden misogyny in storytelling.

- The message is everything to you. Up there, loud and clear.

- Equality and truth are fundamental principles to you, and your stories always reflect this.

- You believe men can be victims of negative masculine regimes as much as women can be corrupted by the patriarchy.

- You want to give a voice to those who have none.

- You relate to the principles of 1970s radical feminism, and the "third wave" feminism of today. You aren't afraid to call yourself a feminist. You're proud!

FIGHTING FEMININITY CHARACTER CASE STUDY:
Wadjda in *Wadjda*

Wadjda is a Saudi Arabian teenage girl who has a simple dream of getting her own bicycle so she can race her best friend, a boy her age. She goes to great lengths to obtain and save enough money, utilizing her considerable skills in coercing, bluffing, and wheeler-dealing. Her childlike state refuses to acknowledge that her dream is impossible in a world where adult women can't leave the house without an escort, and aren't allowed to drive. As Wadjda goes about her quest, she encounters conflict from the two women central to her life: her mother, who despairs of her wayward daughter and fears for her; and her head teacher, the rigid enforcer of society's rules who torments her pupils with the ever-constant threat of the religious police.

Wadjda's ambition makes her a Fighting Femininity heroine as she risks going against the rules of society by voicing and acting on her desire. The sense that Wadjda will one day have to comply, at least on the surface, permeates the story, as does our fear that she might be outcast or punished. The older female characters display Familiar Femininity identification by outwardly conforming to the prevailing conditions in their outer lives, but behind closed doors showing flashes of Fighting Femininity as they covertly break the rules. When Wadjda's mother loses her long campaign to prevent her husband from gaining a second wife (so he gets another chance at getting a son, a task at which she's always failed), she cuts off her hair, and banishes him from her life. Now, she can only find joy and happiness in Wadjda, and she will do all she can for her. At last she finally glorifies in her daughter's defiance, and secretly buys the bike for Wadjda.

Other examples of Fighting Femininity include:

A Girl Walks Home Alone at Night: A female vampire is a feminist angel of death, punishing brutish males and helping victims and females who are on the wrong path.

Dear White People: Sam, a black female student, fearlessly takes on the aggressive and racist white patriarchy at her university. While Sam shows plenty of Familiar Femininity by being a typical student — wanting to succeed at college, have a boyfriend, and be concerned for her ill father — she is a courageous and principled activist who takes direct action against racism.

FEMININE SUPERTHEME 4:
Fantasy Femininity

The SuperTheme of Fantasy Femininity is seen in essentially "unreal" female characters that belong to other worlds, where their special powers define their identity and their way of life. The Fantasy Femininity female protagonist will be able to use her powers to do good, do bad, or simply follow her whims. But they can also be her weak spot; they might render her an outsider, or give her a vulnerability. She might have a dark side or Achilles' heel, but she is essentially a strong female who isn't looking for love, or to settle down. Frequently however she might love passionately, sometimes an impossible love, or one that requires a sacrifice she isn't prepared or able to make. Fantasy Femininity characters can have plenty of buddies, allies, friends, and foes. They aren't really seen in the domestic environment; they are out there in the world on magnificent and thrilling adventures and quests. These female characters may experience love, loss, desire, and even family ties, but their otherworldly dimensions give them agency and prowess, and can make them hugely seductive or alienating. They might hide their abnormal gifts by living as "human" a life as possible, but ultimately, it is the power or the gift that defines their core identity and how they relate to the world.

When the story has a male protagonist, Fantasy Femininity female characters can be antagonistic, or they may make mysterious allies. As female-protagonist leads, they often come in the form of superheroes, vampires, ghosts, fairies, aliens, animals, females who have been medicated with something that takes them beyond the bounds of normality, and even robotic operating systems. They can be found in family and adventure genres, which demand the writer create unique, imaginative, and inspirational worlds.

As a writer who depicts Fantasy Femininity:

- ❋ You want to develop an awesome and compelling female character with no bounds and no restrictions on your imagination.

- ❋ To you, a female character should be as noble, sacrificing, and daring as any male hero.

- ❋ You enjoy writing for young audiences, and you want your fantasy female characters to ultimately be good role models, unless they are the antagonist.

- ❋ You like creating female protagonists with powers that are that literally out of this world, and extreme: highly stylized individuals that transcend mortal concerns and limitations at the same time as having some relatable values.

- ❋ You like strong characters who are only victims on the rare occasions they find themselves at their nemesis's mercy or if they suffer a loss of faith in themselves.

- ❋ You enjoy inventing fantasy words with tribes, clans, factions, myths, and legends. The more fantastical the better. You are an avid fan of superheroes, vampires, and zombies.

* In terms of feminism, you believe women are inherently strong and powerful. You show this by creating female strength that is awesome.

FANTASY FEMININITY CASE STUDY:
Jessica Jones (TV series)

In contemporary New York, Jessica Jones is a hard-drinking, cynical loner private investigator who lives life on her own terms. She's got amazing fighting skills due to her incredible superhuman strength and abilities, but as she wants to avoid attention and blend in, she does her best to avoid using them. Jessica has casual sex on her terms (for instance with Luke, her superhuman neighbor), lives in a dump, shows no real interest in her appearance, and is generally in the bad books of the NYPD and her main client, lesbian attorney Jeri. Jessica avoids emotional entanglements and baggage, dwelling in a sour, seedy world. Jessica is no nurturer of anybody, not even herself. Her best friend, TV personality Trish, looks out for Jessica, knowing that she has a tendency to neglect herself. Jessica is most open with Trish, and deeply loves her. Jessica's one fear is that she is a danger to those who love her because she is still a target of her nemesis Kilgrave, an evil and cruel antagonist who can exert mind control that no one can resist.

Other Fantasy Femininity examples include:

Maleficent: Maleficent is a gentle fairy who falls into the dark side after her loved one proves to be a treacherous, selfish, and ultimately cruel human. Rage and bitterness lead Maleficent to unleash her magical powers to take vengeance and close down all communications between her magical world and the human kingdom. She wreaks punishment on the king, the man she once loved, by sending his daughter, Princess Aurora, to sleep forever.

The Huntsman: Winter's War: The sisters depict Fantastic Femininity as females who harness the forces of nature to wreak destruction as they wish. Like Maleficent, these fantastical female creatures also reflect Fecund Femininity (see below) through their connection with and ability to control the natural world.

FEMININE SUPERTHEME 5:
Fecund Femininity

Fecundity is the natural ability to generate life. Similar to fertility, at its most literal it applies to the female sex's ability to gestate and produce offspring. Fecund Femininity is the Super-Theme that links the female protagonist because of her sex (or acquired sex, in the case of transgender characters) to a belief system that associates femininity with life giving, nurturing of young, and all the protective, caring, and life-enhancing energies necessary for healthy growth. She might be in harmony with the circle of life and the natural world, or she may be a character who is motivated to nurture and is good at it due to implied *innate* factors. At its most literal, Fecund Femininity is the *earth mother* in the female protagonist, whether she is fertile or not. It represents her identification with reproduction and nurturing. It can be seen in a female character who experiences pregnancy, birth, and/or mothering with an acute awareness of her hormones, biological drives, and instinctive love (or hate, or somewhere in between) of the life inside her.

Conversely, it can leave the character exposed to judgment and control by others in misogynistic cultures. Feminism in all forms has always been consumed with fighting patriarchal structures' attempts to control women's bodies and reproductive capacities; thus the biggest conflicts for the Fecund Femininity character can often come from negative and overtly patriarchal characters. Female protagonists who are very protective mothers also reflect aspects of Fecund Femininity, particularly if they identify almost completely as "natural moms" who don't easily trust others (sometimes even their husbands/partners) with their kids. Witches, goddesses, elder tribeswomen healers, and females who shun the civilized world to embrace a lifestyle more deeply entwined with nature (and are seen by other characters to have special life-giving skills and knowledge) can be depictions of this type of femininity. Thus it is frequently associated with Fantasy Femininity as well, where female protagonists are not human. It's actually quite rare to find a protagonist purely associated with Fecund Femininity because most female characters, as part of society, reflect Familiar, Feel-Good, or Fighting Femininity as a reflection of their story worlds' dramatic tone. The protagonist who takes herself off to commune with nature is not at all common. The hippie sect can represent forms of Fecund Femininity wherein all the members honor natural processes. However, the demonic biological mother, driven by her warped instincts, is often a feature of supernatural horror films as an antagonist. Fecund Femininity characters can have the power to bring about destruction through their special connection with the cycle of life.

As a writer who depicts Fecund Femininity:

- You want to create a character who is in touch with the natural world and processes *because* that's an essential aspect of femininity for you.

- You like female characters who heal, are intuitive, and compassionate; they make great, natural mothers.

- You have a hunch men and women are essentially different due to biological factors and evolution, and this difference underpins a lot about how both genders function today.

- You have a tendency to instinctively believe women are the more "natural" carers, and better at respecting and conserving life. A woman who is a bad mother seems unnatural to you.

- You can associate masculinity (and men) with hierarchy, aggression, and oppression, but sometimes with better leadership, strategy, and defense.

- You are in awe of the female body, but equally it could fascinate you; you may like to create revolting maternal figures; you might even fear the female body and its processes. You do not shy from depicting the extreme when it comes to biological processes.

- You might have strong interest in all things Gaia, Goddess, the Great Mother, the Divine Feminine. You probably enjoy depictions of the feminine principle in folklore and mythology.

- You are fascinated by the primal forces of nature and the life cycle: birth, life, death, decay, and renewal.

- You aren't that interested in feminism that tackles social and economic discrimination; you're more interested in the power of the female body as a force of nature.

FECUND FEMININITY CASE STUDY:
Admission

Portia is an admissions officer for Princeton University. She's in a dull, childless relationship with academic Mark, believing they are compatible since they are both "simple folk" leading ordinary lives. She has a radical feminist mother, Susannah, who never knew who Portia's father was, and who thinks Portia is a failure in life. Portia's unresolved and secret past wound is that she became pregnant in college and gave the baby up for adoption. But Portia's simple life is jolted when she is confronted with her past. John, a local teacher, tells her that one of his pupils, the genius Jeremiah, is her biological son. Unable to face it, Portia aggressively denies this, and doesn't want anything more to do with John. She also discovers Mark, her partner, has not only been unfaithful and is ready to leave her, he's impregnated another academic and is expecting twins. When John shows her a copy of Jeremiah's birth certificate, Portia finally accepts that he is her son. She begins to identify physical similarities and traits that she and Jeremiah share as further evidence.

Portia's newly unleashed maternal instinct sends her into overdrive, doing all she can to support John through the Princeton application process. She overcompensates in other ways, like meeting his adoptive parents and "thanking" them, buying him toothbrushes when he visits Princeton for an open day, and finally breaking all professional rules and codes of conduct to get him admitted to Princeton. In the meantime, she and John have an affair, only for John's adopted son Nelson to form a strong attachment to Portia — a stable and "boring" person, unlike John, who is a compulsive world traveler and who is planning on moving to Ecuador. Portia succeeds in getting Jeremiah a place, but she is sacked when her boss finds out she cheated. To add to the disaster, she also discovers that Jeremiah is not her son; the birth certificate John had shown her contained an error. Portia falls out with her mom Susannah, telling her about her pregnancy, and the fact she gave the baby up to spare it a terrible upbringing like her own, made worse by never knowing who her father was. When Susannah tells her that not knowing the name of the man on the train is the biggest regret of her life, but Portia was the best thing to come out of it, Portia finally gets the nurturing that she needs from her mother.

Portia's femininity is part Familiar, part Fecund. Her attachment to Jeremiah is like a fertility placebo effect — Portia's wound has prevented her from giving love to or nurturing anybody; she channels it into devotion to the applicants to Princeton. Portia's arc reveals her maternal instinct slowly coming to life again, exposing her deep human need to have children and care for them. Nurturing, or lack of it, is everywhere in the story; she helps John with a cow in labor, she tells her mom to feed her starving dogs, she goes into nurturing overdrive of Jeremiah, she finally contacts the adoption services to say she's be open to contact with her real son. She forms a family with John and Nelson.

Other Fecund Femininity examples include:

Avatar: The Na'vi belong to a species that are more advanced than humans because they respect and live in harmony with the natural world.

What to Expect When You're Expecting: The story follows five couples as they experience pregnancy. Familiar and Feel-Good intermingle with Fecund Femininity as the women's pregnancies affect their bodies and minds (as well as their relationships) in unexpected ways. The need to create life is a powerful drive in female characters with a unifying aspect of Fecund Femininity.

FEMININE SUPERTHEME 6:
Future Femininity

Future Femininity is a complex SuperTheme, seen in the female protagonist who doesn't see her gender as a problem or an obstacle due to her inherent sense of self-worth and equality; she doesn't exist in a world where male power or the patriarchy is oppressive to her. Things are equal and she can do what she wants, living by her own rules, as can all other female characters in the story. If the culture has defined expectations, they are based on equality between the sexes, wherein men and women share the parenting. She often lives in a task-oriented, professional world, and that's where most of her journey takes place. People she relates to are normally associates and partners. Love affairs can be one-night stands, noncommittal or established relationships where the woman wears the pants, or a relationship kept firmly in a story's background. She can have kids, but their existence doesn't define her whole identity or deflect much from her core professional self. Her partner will share the load and help raise the kids. Like loner male characters, the Future Femininity character doesn't let her emotional life take precedent. If she cracks up under the strain, she'll do what's necessary to patch herself up so she can soon get back in the saddle of achievement.

As a writer who depicts Future Femininity:

- You can make a conscious decision to subvert gender roles that your characters take on so that traditional expectations of male and female characters are minimized.

- Your male characters are often nurturing and empathetic without anyone making a big deal out of it.

- Your female characters are interested in outer-world quests of achieving. They tend to have high self-worth.

- Female characters might have a lot of power over men in the story, and it's no big deal for anyone, a non-issue.

- You might aspire to write films that reflect true equality, in a world where gender conflicts have largely been solved and women don't feel the need to reclaim femininity, obsess over it, or fight it.

- You consciously want to avoid conventional representations of femininity.

- Familiar Femininity and Feel-Good Femininity can make you cringe.

- You simply want to write a story with a strong woman in a "gender neutral" world, or at least a world where your female protagonist doesn't feel like she has to define herself or conform to other people's expectations.

- Your take on femininity, if any, is as a by-product of your story, and not a driving concern.

- You feel that feminism is now mainstream, and equality has arrived for most people living in democratic societies.

FUTURE FEMININITY CASE STUDY:
Carrie Mathison in *Homeland*

Another long-running series, *Homeland*, gives us a female protagonist in Carrie Mathison who is representative of both Future Femininity and Familiar Femininity. Carrie is affected by bipolar mental-health issues, which help and hinder her job as a CIA agent. She is driven by her compulsive need to get the job done, whatever the risks to her safety or mental health. (This becomes less so as the series progresses.) Carrie has close relationships with men, such as her also-bipolar father, and her handler Saul, who understands that she is one of the best operatives he's ever worked with despite her sometimes unorthodox methods of investigation. He also knows her weaknesses, such as her addiction to risk, and her commitment to finding out the truth by following her intuition.

Abandoned by her mother, Carrie has developed no real need for women friends or emotional support. Carrie has no particularly strong bonds with women, other than with her older sister who attempts to be a grounding influence when Carrie's manic episodes kick in. She is capable of strong attachments to men, as her ongoing affair with potentially "turned" soldier Brody demonstrates, but not if it may come at the expense of her job, which towers above all else. It is only in the later seasons, when Carrie becomes a single mother, that she identifies with Familiar Femininity, where a character's kids top her priorities. She aspires to give her daughter normalcy by leaving the agency and working for an aid organization — but when she becomes the target of terrorists, she has to return to her old life so she can crack the case and protect her daughter's life. As a mother and a professional, she is torn.

Other examples of Future Femininity include:

Elementary: Joan Watson, as Sherlock's partner, is an interesting reflection of Future and Familiar Femininity. She is completely committed to her work as an investigator, having lost faith in her ability as a medical surgeon. She has no interest in a typical relationship or becoming a mother; she is happy to live unconventionally with Sherlock platonically. True to the Watson/Sherlock lineage, the bond they have as partners is unbreakable; Joan looks out for Sherlock as much as he does for her. She isn't looking for love, particularly, and she might feel claustrophobic in relationships with men — they get in the way of her true calling to work with Sherlock. When she discovers she has a half-sister, Lin Wen, Watson's family wounds are reopened, arousing her curiosity about her estranged father.

SUPERTHEME 7:
Felonious Femininity

Felonious Femininity is most often found in the female anti-hero due to her inherent and absolute identification with criminality and/or dark drives. Rarer than her male counter-parts, this female character identifies as a misanthrope who simply hates the human race, and is somewhat motivated to do harm to others. As a protagonist, she is the female character who identifies with nothing but her own needs, obsessions, and moral code. Her hostility to others may be targeted mainly at men, but occasionally at women as well. The Felonious Femininity character has no ideals beyond self-gratification and her private moral code that benefits nobody but herself, and those she "loves." Her love can be maternal, overprotective, compulsive, or controlling of others. She sees no point in fighting the system for change when she can achieve her own ends by her own means, however immoral. She is a law unto herself, a loner, a cynic, and a trickster all in one. In both male and female-driven films and shows, Felonious Femininity is found more often in female antagonists. As protagonist, she could be the female equivalent of Dexter, Tony Soprano, Hannibal, or Gregory House: charismatic and compulsive misanthropes with little allegiance to morality who dwell mainly on the dark side. Why she hasn't yet entered the mainstream in substantial numbers is largely because this type of femininity presses all the old buttons of fear about inherently bad women who are out for themselves and nobody else.

The female character who identifies with Felonious Femininity is everything girls are brought up *not* to be — greedy, insatiable, cunning, cynical, selfish, go-getting, and twisted. So she sometimes risks being softened in the writing process by focusing on her positive attributes, such as loving her children, mending her ways, falling in love, or ending up punished or dead. Felonious Femininity at its purest represents the pathological narcissist in the female character, her drive for personal power and a personal agenda to live by. She may be overtly or secretly criminal. Games and deception are hugely important factors in her *modus operandi*. She was either born bad or made bad; it doesn't really matter which because she's beyond hope, often not suffering for her choices. If she embraces any redemption, it will be her choice alone. She may kill out of hate, or to achieve her own ends. She may be self-destructive and self-hating underneath it all, but her story is seldom about healing her inner wounds. Empathy can sometimes be created for the Felonious Femininity character by backstory that shows how she was made bad, normally by suffering unspeakable abuse from others. Internal conflicts don't drive her, since her psyche has largely shut these down. She doesn't experience guilt. External conflicts come from her multiple enemies.

As a writer who depicts Felonious Femininity:

- ✤ You enjoy creating dark and twisted female characters.
- ✤ You believe it's high time for bad female protagonists to be celebrated, and want to balance the numbers to match those of morally complex male characters.
- ✤ You may be a misanthrope at heart, or at times... the inherent evil of people fascinates you. In your darker moments you believe all people are greedy, pathetic, and self-serving.
- ✤ You find redemptive stories are unbelievable, unrealistic, and overly predictable.
- ✤ You are up for the fight in defending your female protagonist, and know she is going to push other people's buttons.

- Violent female characters appeal to you as much as violent male characters. You have no problem with women being sadistic or vicious.

- You want to create a female who gets away with it, and we love her for it. You give her lots of POV!

- You like morally ambiguous themes in your writing.

- You aren't convinced female solidarity is viable in a world where dog eats dog.

- You are too cynical to believe feminism will make a better world for women, who can be just as corrupt as men.

FELONIOUS FEMININITY CASE STUDY:
Amy Dunne in *Gone Girl*

Amy is educated, intelligent, and beautiful, on the surface a perfect wife. Deep down, Amy loathes and detests her weak "loser" of a husband Nick for dragging her away from her sophisticated life to be a bored housewife in a dull town so he may be near his dying mother, wasting her trust fund income. Amy feels superior to Nick to the point of pure hatred. He disgusts her. She is a loner with no friends. When she discovers the ultimate insult to her — that Nick has had an affair — she decides to make him pay the price by framing him for her kidnapping and murder. Her narcissistic sense of self has been fed by her parents who were more in love with the idea of their only child and golden-girl daughter as a character in a bestselling series of children's books than with the real Amy. Leaving a trail of sophisticated clues that lead to Nick's arrest, Amy goes on the run. She is gleeful and triumphant at the hell into which she has plunged Nick and his sister. When things don't go as planned on her escape mission,

Amy's criminal mind kicks in again. This time, she frames an old boyfriend (who once stalked her) for kidnapping and raping her. Yet again, her public personality is believed and she is returned safely home to Nick, who now knows he has married a monster. Amy's strategic mind, cold cunning, and utter disgust for those she considers inferior are compelling inner drives to make the world bend to her will, whenever and however she deems fit.

Other examples of Fatal Femininity include:

Justified: Mags Bennett, in Season 2. As a matriarch of a highly dysfunctional and criminal Kentucky hillbilly family, Mags is a drug-dealing mastermind and murderer.
Black Swan: Vulnerable ballerina Nina discovers she can only achieve her ambitions by fully embracing her dark side.

Feminine SuperThemes in One Character

The SuperThemes model can help you think about all the ways you relate to versions of femininity through your characters. Much like how we, as writers, recognize our own gender to be a shifting, complicated, neverending entity, characters' relationship with *their* gender can be equally complex and multilayered. Therefore, the vast majority of female characters can reflect several different SuperThemes. It's not a bad thing for some female protagonists to clearly associate with one SuperTheme if it works perfectly fine for both the story and the dramatic function she has. Other characters display a combination, either as part of their arc, or just because they are highly complex and reflect the boundless ways female characters negotiate gender, just as real women do! It's not uncommon for a Familiar Femininity character to reflect Fighting Femininity as she encounters sexual inequality or discrimination in some form. The mother in *Wadjda* goes from being a protective, law-abiding caregiver to a covert feminist who will support her daughter's dreams. Some Familiar Femininity characters share Fantasy Femininity. In *The Babadook*, Amelia is a single mother experiencing bereavement, her partner having died on the same day that her son was born. As her battle with the Babadook, a creature from a storybook, takes on monstrous proportions, Amelia becomes fantastical herself and definitely reflects both Fecund and Felonious Femininity aspects in her protective rage and violence. She even tells her child how much he disgusts her at one point. She also has tones of Fighting Femininity as she grows in power, standing up to a bitchy group of wives and finally defining a happy life with her son on her own terms, managing her own internal demons.

On TV, Vanessa Ives in *Penny Dreadful* reflects Familiar Femininity, Fighting Femininity, Future Femininity, and Fantasy Femininity. She is Familiar in her mild-mannered and polite bearing as a respectable Victorian young woman, with a value system of caring for those she loves and generally does right by. She is plagued by guilt over the death of her best friend Mina, who was taken by vampires. Another female character, Joan Clayton, the Cut-Wife, is a reclusive white witch and abortionist to the local village women; she gives Vanessa a deeper understanding of her own dark side. Together they represent Fighting Femininity and Fecund Femininity. They form a symbolic mother/daughter relationship when the Cut-Wife shows Vanessa how to use her powers. The Cut-Wife reflects aspects of Fecund Femininity in the passing on of witch lore to Vanessa. When the villagers attack the Cut-Wife's home and burn her at the stake, Vanessa is spared, yet branded a witch with a red-hot iron, an atrocity that scars her back. This motivates her to mark the Cut-Wife's home as her own as a pledge of allegiance against the evil sorority of witches who serve the Devil. As a target of fallen angels, Vanessa reflects Fantasy Femininity as a possessed, crazily deranged woman who is locked up and subjected to oppressive treatment for "her own good." Only Vanessa knows the evil she is facing. If she loses the battle, she will be overtaken and beyond redemption. Those who love her come to realize she is fighting a battle with Dracula, who is attracted to her inherently dark powers and seeks her as his bride.

Ensemble casts in TV with a range of female protagonists can show a blend of all the SuperThemes, such as *Girls*, *Game of Thrones*, and *Orange Is the New Black*.

Female comediennes like Amy Schumer, Catherine Tate, and Tracey Ullman mash the SuperThemes up with a hilarious range of feminists, victims, oddballs, and weirdos. Schumer's females are Familiar Femininity heroines who encounter the sexual double standard in all walks of life, frequently to the bemusement and befuddlement of the female character being played by Schumer. Female characters are also targeted — to invert stereotypes and to make fun of women who make themselves pathetic, frequently sending up extreme forms of femininity as ridiculous. Schumer uses spoof situations and surreal nightmare scenarios in a Fighting Femininity tone.

⟶ *EXERCISE* ⟵
Self-Assessment

Let's think about you and your motivations for choosing a female protagonist, and what kinds of gender issues your story will explore. On the next page, you'll see a Self-Assessment Questionnaire to complete. This is the first of many that appear throughout this book. Most of them are going to be addressed to your character, but some will be addressed to you.

Even if you don't have a writing project on the go at the moment, still try to fill them in.

⟶ SCREENWRITER'S SUPERTHEME QUESTIONNAIRE ⟵

1. Why do you want to write this story?
2. Who do you think your audience is? What SuperTheme would best describe the women who would see your film/show?
3. If you could choose five adjectives to describe the situation of women in your culture, what would they be?
4. What are some of your favorite films with female protagonists? Why do you like these female protagonists?
5. Do any of the Feminine SuperThemes feel particularly relevant to the female-led films being produced in your culture?
6. If any film with a female protagonist particularly annoys you, can you say why?
7. If you have a project on the go, do you think any of the SuperThemes are influencing you? How?
8. Writing with a male protagonist? Try to work out how he relates to the Feminine SuperThemes. How does he identify with gender expectations?

CHAPTER 2

Going Against Type:
The M-Factor

Now it's time to think about who your female protagonist is going to be, and why. Why choose her? What's
so special about her? Why does she appeal to you? There is a
good chance, if you are writing a project, that you may already
know who your character is. She might be based on a true-life
story of someone you know or admire; she could be a thinly
disguised version of you! She might be someone completely
fictional, invented by your originality. Alternatively, she might
be a fusion of all these things, influenced by who you are,
the women you know, other screen heroines, and your own
wild imagination.

Most of us set out to create a kind of truth in a female
protagonist, alongside bringing something new, something
we've never seen a female character be or do before. It's that
novelty element, whether it is a personality trait, a problem
she faces, or a choice she makes, which gives her a memorable, unique quality. Whoever she is, your aim is to create

a protagonist who will launch thousands of viewers to their screens and will keep them there, gripped and entertained. They want to see a memorable character telling a story that might be true to life, but which is described in a way they have never seen or heard.

The audience will use the information you give about your protagonist to make immediate assessments about her. It's a human need to "place" a person as quickly as possible so we can start to relate to them and know where we stand. We root out recognizable factors in character; even when we watch a world movie, from an entirely different culture, we look out for themes, characters, and stories that might bear out or validate our own understanding and experience of life.

Likewise, each member of the audience will relate your character to their own external and internal experiences of "what women are like" and the roles that the female characters are or are not associated with. "External" means the women they have met and related to in their own lives. "Internal" means the idealized images or negative projections we carry around about females that are shaped by our own personal experiences.

So it's your job to make her stand out, even if she is associated with certain types and roles.

Choosing a Character

As we all have to start somewhere, choose a female protagonist now, however embryonic she might be at this stage, and begin developing her using some of the following strategies and exercises. You can then move on to flesh out her story. By the time you've gotten to the last page of this book, your character and your story will have gone through a huge number of changes. You will have fresh insights, new inspirations, and hopefully bigger and better ideas. That's the whole point of rewriting and development, and reading books like this one!

So don't fret if you have a tendency to be commitment-phobic with your characters. She will grow on the job, or fail spectacularly.

If you've written many stories, you probably know that all your characters go through monumental transformations each time you rewrite scenes, sequences, or full drafts. A female protagonist can change her voice and her attitude from scene to scene. On a bad day, it can seem you are subjecting your character to a series of brain transplants; or, in a worst-case scenario, a frontal lobotomy. And when your screenplay goes into a development process that has to take into account the creative input of others, let's just say the number of surgeons and diagnoses only increases. But ultimately your character is your patient. It is your job to heal her based on the notes and guidance of others as well as your creative instincts.

⟶ *Exercise* ⟶
Finding Your Female Protagonist

So why is this strange female creature lurking in your subconscious? I'm sure there are many others suitable for the job of leading your screenplay, so what is it about this one?

Let her tell you. She's got to fill out the *Application Questionnaire for the Role of Female Protagonist* on the next page.

The purpose of this exercise is to bring your protagonist into existence. She's not carved in stone, and you may abandon her yet. Over the remainder of this book, you will get lots of chances to develop your characterization. Think of it like training her — and yourself — on the job. You and your character are forming a team, learning from each other.

⟿ APPLICATION QUESTIONNAIRE ⟿
for the Role of Female Protagonist

1. What is your name? Any nicknames? How do you feel about your name?

2. Why do you want to lead this screenplay?

3. What do you feel you can bring to the role?

4. Why would audiences like you? For your strengths, or your weaknesses? Why might they dislike you? What's your dark side?

5. Give me three reasons why I should give this job to you and not to anyone else.

6. What are your personal goals and objectives for the future? Do you expect to achieve any of these during this screenplay?

7. Are you married, single, or divorced? If married or single, are you happy about that? If divorced, what went wrong? Are any issues from your past relationship going to get in the way?

8. Do you have children? If yes, do they live with you? Do you expect them to accompany you in this story? What childcare needs will you have?

9. Where do you live? Describe your neighborhood. Why do you live there? Are you planning to travel or relocate in the course of the screenplay?

10. What is your current occupation and salary?

11. What are your notable achievements? Might the audience have already heard of you? Are you famous, or celebrated?

12. Finally, if you were a car, what car would you be? Why?

Now that you've chosen your character, it's time to consider her dimensionality.

Creating Dimension

Creating a distinctive female character forces you to develop dimension in multiple ways, whether you are aware of it or not. Nobody wants to create a bland female character, but unless we are aware of some of the risks attached to female protagonists, we might! Let's think about what could make a bland female protagonist.

- She's just like too many other characters we've seen time and time again.
- She's a stereotype with little dimension.
- She doesn't threaten traditional values or expectations.
- She might have no personality, but she could be super-hot, or surrounded by huge action and adventure.
- She doesn't work things out for herself; other characters (particularly male ones) do the thinking and decision-making for her. She very often has little to zero POV.
- She can often be saved, mainly by men, or by other memorable female characters.
- She's really relatable, a regular human being who we admire.

If you are committed to making her as compelling as possible, the "Dimensionality Diagram" below might be helpful. It shows some of the factors influencing characterization during the writing process, and can function as an overarching framework for character building. Looking at them, ask yourself if you actively consider these when you're creating a female character.

The Dimensionality Diagram

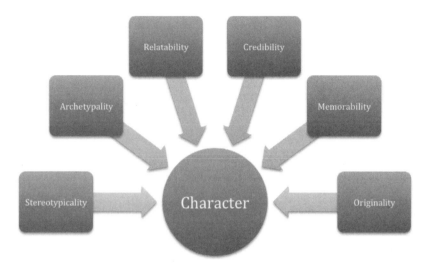

Let's take a look at the elements of the Dimensionality Diagram.

Stereotypicality

The most readymade way of helping the audience connect to the character is by using stereotypes, the most two-dimensional and clichéd form of characterization. Stereotypes and stereotypical behavior can and do have uses, particularly in comedies. The overprotective and/or competitive mother, or the ball-breaking female boss, can be funny depending on your taste and the context.

Female characterization can still reflect "old school" stereotypes, especially in male-driven genre movies. Some of these include:

- The helpless female who needs saving
- the superhot girl who just wants to have fun with guys
- the beautiful young girl who never gets angry or behaves badly and is worthy of being saved

- the slut who gets punished
- the Gorgon female boss or law-enforcement officer
- the nagging wife
- the nagging mother
- the tart with a heart
- the bitchy gang of girls
- the ugly nerd/best-friend girl
- the "flibbertigibbet" weird, wacky, or nerdy girl

We all know them. Whether you love or hate to write them will depend very firmly on how you want to represent your female characters and why. It all boils down to your intentions for your story, its genre, its tone, its style, and your themes. Using stereotypes is a bit like shopping in a cut-price clothes shop full of mass-produced versions of this season's styles. Bargain doesn't have to mean bad — stereotypes can go the distance and have a lot of value in terms of "instant gratification." You can be lazy and buy a complete "ready to wear, disposable wardrobe" with no effort on your part. Or you can blend the familiar with the original — such as by mixing new clothes with vintage. You can buy the cheap, mass-produced dress but then you customize it. By choosing an off-the-peg character, you can make her original with lots of unique traits. Or you can simply walk on by and choose bespoke. It can be fun to write a stereotypical female character who ends up evolving quite unexpectedly.

Female stereotypes or stereotypical traits in *female-driven* stories can include:

- Angry/failed female cop
- The beautiful/better female rival to the protagonist

- The judgmental/bitchy group of caryatids who don't include the protagonist
- The best friend who lets the protagonist down
- The beautiful and successful best friend who has everything
- The granny who speaks words of wisdom
- Good mothers for whom family always comes first
- The female protagonist whose soulmate is conveniently extremely good looking and very wealthy
- The rivalrous mother-in-law/daughter-in-law or sisters
- Man-hating feminists

Archetypality

Archetypes are generally accepted as aspects of the human self that have evolved across millennia. They have a kind of recurring truth and are found in similar forms across most human societies. Archetypes are based on the principle that certain recognizable roles are a result of human existence, and emerge out of a collective unconscious. They are seen as masks that we wear and that are interchangeable. Carl Jung and Joseph Campbell explored the function of archetypes, and Vogler's *The Writer's Journey* utilizes these to generate a system of archetypes useful for building characters. Conventional feminine archetypes from fairy tales and myths include:

- The wise woman
- The wicked stepmother
- The powerful witch/sorceress
- The virgin

- The protective mother
- The jealous wife
- The vulnerable maiden

However, Jungian feminists such as Maureen Murdock, Clarissa Pinkola Estés, and Linda Leonard explore "female" or "feminine" archetypes that have their own distinctive roles and attributes, and relate more directly to their understanding of female psychology and patterns in embodying the experiences consistently determined by gender and culture.

To what extent you believe in deep archetypal patterns in humanity (masculine, feminine, or simply human) is your call. You may believe some feminine archetypes, like the ones listed above, are products of a patriarchal way of defining women's lives across the centuries. As a writer, you might enjoy reflecting on your characters with any of these types or models. They may inspire new insights, or not be helpful at all. How your imagination engages with them is probably beyond your control anyway! When it comes to your female protagonist, you can decide if you feel these are shaping her "innate" being or her soul. The risk remains that without distinctive and complex characterization, she might feel rather stereotypical. In addition, feminine archetypes don't help you question or explore the story world's specific culture, political situation, economics, or gender roles, all of which may be affecting your female character.

Relatability

Choosing aspects of your female protagonist that make her relatable to the audience can be a tricky process. If you don't work on her memorability, you may risk her being an acceptable cliché. An acceptable cliché is one step up from the off-the-peg stereotype. Acceptable clichés are the female characters (protagonists or secondary characters) who might have some complexity, but not enough to make them truly memorable. Some obvious "acceptable cliché" character types include:

- The depressed/needy mother who wants more contact with her adult children

- The protagonist who is insecure about her looks or failures

- The strong career woman who is conflicted by the demands and needs of her family

- The strong action female protagonist who is young and beautiful with an unresolved past wound

- The ball-breaking loner or cynic who is secretly sad and lonely

- The bubbly female who is oriented toward men's attention and approval but who lacks self-esteem

- The lonely single mom of the female protagonist that she is somehow compensating for

If any of these feel similar to your characters, several factors could be influencing you. Firstly, you might really believe these are if not true at least familiar to women's real experiences. Secondly, you might fear making a female character too dark or originally difficult, because you believe audiences want female characters to conform. Thirdly, you don't want to face the complexity of female psychology because you'd rather not fully engage with or understand female identity issues. Finally, you might not have a particularly feminist stance.

Making a character relatable doesn't always depend on using types. You can also give your female protagonist a familiar problem that "being female" can attract. So now the "type" is placed on the problem, not the character, and the problem can be an acceptable cliché. You can make her response to this problem as generic or as individual as you wish. Again, without having a really good sense of who she is as a unique human being, you can risk her being overly familiar in the way she handles life and its problems.

The common approach to relatability is giving the female character an identity and experiences that fall into the Familiar Femininity SuperTheme, alongside a personality that is admirable. Admirable character traits are those that "most" people would consider strengths, such as being unselfish, docile, caring, considerate, sensible, practical, patient, sensitive to others, and even reserved.

Credibility

Is it important to you that the audience believes in your character? Or do you want to push the boundaries by creating a character who does totally extreme/unpredictable things, and you don't care if the audience is with her or not? It might be that you choose to take a "type" of female character who has some elements of "acceptable cliché" but you give her a really extreme adventure/problem. For example, a seventy-five-year-old granny pulling off a major bank-robbery heist. In this case you are out to subvert the acceptable cliché, push the boundaries of relatability, and open the audience's mind by creating new possibilities for older female protagonists. It might be that you are truly motivated to create a female protagonist who is credible to you, and if *you* believe her, that is enough.

Credibility is possibly behind the growing number of female protagonists that reflect real women's achievements on screen. These characters give us a far broader range of experiences and identities true to women's achievements and aspirations. Some of these include:

- Women as politicians or political players

- Women as leaders

- Mothers as career women

- Single women as professional women

- Older women having romances

- Sportswomen

- Women warriors

- Females working together in business

- Disadvantaged girls trying to make a difference

- Fairy-tale female characters showing they are very different than the stereotypes!

Remember, credible doesn't necessarily mean relatable. Sometimes a credible female character is tricky to understand or like, or you may fear that she will be. This can bring you back to the eternal questions and dilemmas for writers about likeability, and how far you want to push the boundaries.

Memorability

Who is going to remember your female protagonist and why? We remember characters for very personal and subjective reasons, but when we think about standout female protagonists, we're often talking about ones that have gone the distance — certainly in terms of being known and talked about. Memorability in your female protagonist could include:

- She has an *M-Factor* — a unique quality that is unforgettable (see below)

- She pushes the boundaries, either in her life or as a person. She's a force to be reckoned with, even if she doesn't start out as one.

- She drives the action and dominates the scenes she's in. We can't take our eyes off her; we are rooting for her.

- Her story is gripping and compelling because we understand and empathize with what is at stake for her.

- She reflects a Feminine SuperTheme or two in an original and distinctive way.

- She has a certain amount of dysfunction. Things aren't alright for her. She doesn't know how to handle the conflict and jeopardy in which life is placing her.

- She may divide the audience in terms of likable and unlikable traits.

- She isn't at all stereotypical. She's not two-dimensional; she's multifaceted.

Originality

You might believe you have a duty to create original characters by stretching and pushing your imagination and writing to the best of your ability. With so many female characters being plagued by typecasting, originality demands you to pay real attention to the decisions you are making in the writing process, and to be able to articulate your intentions for your characters when working with others. Sometimes originality boils down to having a memorable female character addressing a familiar problem. But even better is a memorable female character with a memorable problem. The problem will be made even more original by the other characters and the distinctive world you create.

Brainstorm some female characters you know and place them into the following categories:

- ⚜ the most **despised** (in that her personality, values, or actions may alienate you, although you might be utterly gripped by her)

- ⚜ the most **admired** (a character who deeply inspires you by what they stand for)

- ⚜ the most **memorable** (a character who you have never forgotten for some distinctive way of being)

It's a fun exercise, and better to do in a group. What you will come away with is a series of extremely passionate comments about which famous character falls into which category. Try not to fall out!

Here are some of mine:

Despised — Skyler (*Breaking Bad*), Cersei (*Game of Thrones*), Mags Bennett (*Justified*), Figueroa (*Orange Is the New Black*).
Admired — Precious (*Precious*), Katniss (*The Hunger Games*), Hayes Morrison (*Conviction*), Joy (*Joy*), Joan Watson (*Elementary*), Peggy (*Mad Men*), Christy (*Mom*), Wadjda (*Wadjda*).
Memorable — Maleficent (*Maleficent*), Mags Bennett (*Justified*), the whole gang of inmates (*Orange Is the New Black*), Vanessa Ives (*Penny Dreadful*), P.L. Travers (*Saving Mr. Banks*), Bonnie (*Mom*), Betty (*Mad Men*), vampire (*A Girl Walks Home Alone at Night*).

Scarlett O'Hara from *Gone With the Wind*, with all her petulance, self-seeking, feistiness, determination, and positivity, is a female protagonist that has truly gone the distance and still manages to feel contemporary eighty years on! She has a standout, impulsive selfishness that is childish yet relatable. She won't crumble when the chips are down.

Selfishness makes her determined and indomitable, yet utterly frustrating.

The Memorability Factor

Let's start thinking about the ways you can make your character *memorable*. To help you, I'd like to introduce you to a concept called the *M-Factor*. Your character's M-Factor (shorthand for Memorability Factor) is her incredibly unique and unforgettable quality, one that has never been seen before. Okay, she might have a couple of very interesting qualities; this exercise will make sure you have at least one!

The M-Factor will:

- Inspire your writing of the screenplay, causing you to jump out of bed each morning and race to the laptop
- Make your character stand out to script readers who can only recommend her to others, including decision-makers like producers or directors
- Intrigue producers and make them sleep uncomfortably at night if they reject her, or be excited to be giving her a shot
- Make an actor want to bring her to life
- Make her reach wide audiences over decades who will never forget her!

The M-Factor Equation

Here's a really simple equation to find your heroine's M-Factor.

M-Factor = your protagonist's compulsive need + most shocking/difficult trait x charismatic or endearing quality.

Let's apply it to Scarlett O'Hara.

Scarlett's M-Factor = self-seeking (*compulsive need*) + outrageous manipulation (*shocking trait*) x optimistic determination (*charismatic trait*).

Scarlett's M-Factor = Ruthless prima donna

Remember that the M-Factor has nothing to do with how sympathetic your character is, or how "likable." This is not the place to worry about alienating the audience. She needs to be *complex*, but not necessarily *nice*.

⌐ *Exercise* ⌐
Work Out the M-Factor for Your Female Protagonist

Ask yourself what aspects of your character people might find despicable, admirable, and likable. Brainstorm these.

Do the M-Factor equation above and see what you come up with! Don't worry if you surprise or even shock yourself. You can always change it when further character and story development give you bigger and better insights.

Once you've found your character's M-Factor, use it as a metaphoric touchstone to recall her core self if notes and feedback send you off-base. It will always bring you back.

A Memorable Story

Once you have found your character's M-Factor, you will eventually have to give it a story that illuminates it brilliantly. The best way is to put your character in a situation where her M-Factor is sorely tested. By putting her M-Factor under pressure, your character will learn which aspects of her personality are helping her grow and which aspects are holding her back. Remember: the M-Factor is not the same as a negative personality trait that has to change, but there is a good chance that one aspect of her M-Factor will undergo a transformation. This is the side of your character that gets her into trouble.

Scarlett O'Hara's M-Factor: By the end of her long story, during which she is sorely tested, Scarlett does not give up her ebullient determination. She is never going to be a truly altruistic being. But she might think twice about playing any more games with Rhett if she really wants to get him back.

A Further Word On Likeability

Nowadays, we generally strive to create female protagonists to be non-stereotypical, unless we are having fun; we make them responsible for their problems, and we want to see them fight for themselves, learn lessons, overcome barriers, and stand up to threats — just like any male protagonist. As mentioned, some writers may be still disinclined to create the truly difficult female protagonist, the darker "anti-heroine" whose badness the audience is encouraged to celebrate. Perhaps audiences just have not yet warmed to celebrating bad female protagonists enough that they can begin rooting for truly non-remorseful or non-punished bad girls as "anti-heroines." In an equal world, the morality of our characters should be gender blind, but it often isn't, particularly when it comes to the female protagonist. If you feel compelled to soften your female protagonist because you feel it is too difficult to write a morally deficient or deeply conflicted female, try examining your deeper motivations and concerns.

Consider all the dark, complex male heroes that have entertained and compelled millions in recent years. When it comes to men, the more complex, wounded, and alienated, the better. Darkness and moral ambiguity are fine for these antiheroes. To what extent you keep alert to a sex or gender double standard when creating characters is ultimately your choice, but nobody can pretend these still don't exist! For instance, you may feel you need to generate huge levels of sympathy for your character to justify any difficult choices she might make. Remember that the roots of this double standard are to be found in our earliest life experiences and our expectations about women's behavior. There are plenty of tough, hardnosed, tricky girls and women out there, but how easy are they for you to write?

Remember that many female protagonists still risk being oversoftened or typecast. They drown in the *sea of mediocrity* because they simply aren't complex enough.

Remember Scarlett.

⌒ *EXERCISE* ⌒
Who, Why, How?

This exercise gets you to think objectively about your female character, warts and all!

1. Brainstorm all the different sorts of people who might encounter your protagonist, such as women, men, friends, fellow students, family, script readers, producers, directors, your target audience.

2. Ask yourself, alongside each group, "What might they find difficult about her? Do I care about their opinion? And if I do, why does it matter?" This kind of reflection may help you work out what your priorities for your protagonist really are, and the reasons why. You can draw a big heart over the people or groups whose opinion you really care about.

3. You can highlight the main traits or character features that spring out at you.

4. Reflect on the ways you might want to change your character for your favorite people/target groups.

Wrapping Up...

By now, you should have identified both who your female protagonist is, and have a good idea about her M-Factor. You are hopefully feeling emboldened enough to make her complex and not just "good." Now it's time to think about the Role-Choices your female protagonist identifies with.

CHAPTER 3

Making It Personal:
Using Role-Choices

Your female protagonist will have made certain choices about life when she walks onto page one of your screenplay (or not too long after). It's up to you to decide what those choices are, and how they are going to either change during her story, or be cemented in her sense of identity. By using them creatively, you can illuminate both your character's individuality, as well as the specific nature of the culture she lives within.

The trouble for some female protagonists is that they might want to do their own thing, and find that the roles they have to assume don't meet their needs very well. In this way, these roles can take a toll on your female character, depending on her personality, her family, and the culture. She might, for instance, have real trouble integrating herself or even wanting to belong due to gender roles and societal expectations.

Thinking about your character's "Role-Choices" will help you make a better judgment call on what is a recognizable and truthful aspect to her individual character, and what can be a cliché. The Role-Choice system is a typological approach based on kinds of roles that characters identify with. Reflecting on Role-Choices that you associate with your character asks you to consider how and why you are consciously and subconsciously associating your character with expectations of females in her or your own culture. Using them this way can help you ensure your character is unique, recognizing that a female character in the story usually triggers some pretty powerful unconscious feelings in the audience when it comes to stereotypically female "roles." Remember, the whole point of a Role-Choice is to help you question the whole notion of "types." If someone says your character is a "maternal type," it could mean that you have emphasized in her character an over-identification with the Nurturing Role-Choice, specifically the Mother. If this wasn't your intention, you may need to look at her traits, actions, and attitudes. Then you can examine your own unconscious agenda in terms of gender roles that could be playing out through your character.

> *A Role-Choice is your character's conscious and unconscious relationship to cultural expectations of women's societal roles. It's a way of reflecting on how she wants to be defined, how she defines herself, and how others define her.*

How to Use Role-Choices

The main aim of the Role-Choices is to *help you work out how your character, as an individual, relates to any given Role-Choice.* The more you enter her mind, the more you will understand how her individuality makes her choose what she chooses, and do the things she does. A stereotype and archetype can only go so far. A Role-Choice asks you to define your character's choices and the reasons for them, taking her culture and other factors into account. What does this role mean in the culture and world of the story? What does it mean to your character and her sense of identity? Is it a help or a hindrance?

A Role-Choice affects your character's internal and external sense of identity. One way of thinking about Role-Choices is by relating them to stages we go through in life, when we identify with certain ways of being. It's like when people say things like, *"That was when I was into being an earth mother"* or *"that's when I was playing happy families"* or *"that's when I was trying to be a better mother than my own mom."* It's the *"when I was being..."* bit of the Statement that reflects what a Role-Choice is, and how your character might identify with it, unique to her. As you get to know each Role-Choice, imagine your character is very old, looking back on her life. How would she remember the roles she took on?

A Role-Choice isn't a job or actual vocation either. Your character's attitude toward certain Role-Choices may result in her choosing a certain kind of job (or being stuck with no option but to do a certain kind of job), but a Role-Choice is much broader. It's about her whole identity and self-perception as a woman both internally and externally.

A Role-Choice can help you to question and explore your female protagonist's attitudes to her world, her place within it, and how she wants to be identified (even if she learns that this isn't helpful to her). In this respect, you can use a Role-Choice to question certain expectations about women, and how they play out in the world, and what your character feels about them. How your character relates to each Role-Choice is a way you can deepen your characterization *and* your story. Remember, they can make you question your own feelings and views about why women make certain Role-Choices.

It is most likely that as the story develops, so will your character's Role-Choices. She might strongly identify with certain Role-Choices at the start of her story that she will gradually grow out of. She might start identifying with others in new and exciting ways as her identity changes. The Role-Choice can last the whole story long or be momentary, visible in a scene or two. Your character can identify with any Role-Choice at any given moment in a way that is true to her. It isn't a fixed, unwavering system.

You might decide that certain Role-Choices will only be evident in other female characters to serve as a reminder of what your heroine could be if conditions or her attitudes change or don't change. Seeing a way of being in other women, for example, might make her reject that particular Role-Choice because it's the last thing she wants to be identified with. Or another character will make a certain Role-Choice, and be a good example or good "role model" for your protagonist. Sometimes it can be helpful to do a mapping exercise by brainstorming which characters may be clearly associated with which Role-Choices and *how* they are identifying with them. This can help you explore some of your unconscious associations between roles, sex, and gender.

Remember, Role-Choices are a creative approach to support your writing choices. So use them flexibly. There's no right or wrong.

The Feminine Role-Choices

The Role-Choices are presented in two groups, the "feminine" and the "masculine," these being the main types of roles frequently associated with these genders in many cultures. Many females spend a lot of time in real life dealing with what is expected from them in terms of cultural "femininity," and you can see this reflected in many female-driven stories. By associating them with masculine Role-Choices, writers are also increasingly consciously subverting the kinds of roles that contribute to their female characters' identities.

You may not like the terms "masculine" and "feminine" regarding your female characters' traits, so you might not like this approach. It might feel too rigid, or like typecasting. But it's still amazing how even the most complicated female characters can still reflect "feminine" Role-Choices. You may prefer to try out using "masculine" Role-Choices to build identity.

The Feminine Role-Choices are grouped into four sets:

* Heroine
* Nurturer
* Dependent
* Believer

Now let's meet each one.

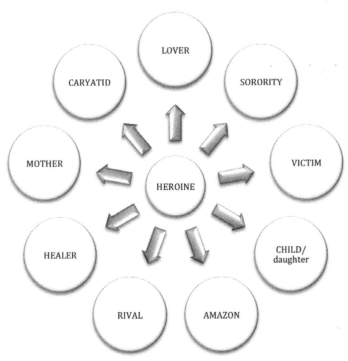

The Role-Choice of Heroine

The Role-Choice of Heroine represents your character finding a sense of identity in relationship to other people. It is the "feminine" sense of self, in that connection with others, in a positive or negative way, that is central to this character's sense of self. It is the part of the self that needs others, which seeks to care for others and be cared for by others, at the same time as making sense of who she is in relation to others. A protagonist does not live in isolation, even if she is alone. She may be alone because others have defined her too much, and it is only by caring for herself that she will heal. Sometimes she will heal and find herself by allowing others to care for her. She is at once *seeking out* who she is, and *reacting to* the impositions that others may place on her, whether that is intentional or not. Essentially, identifying as a Heroine is about coming to terms with oneself in relationship to others. Children may not deliberately want to impose, but they cannot help it, as they have needs. However, the Heroine in your female character may or may not enjoy the bonds of love, particularly if she is trying to find an identity beyond caring. In your story, you are going to narrow down a period in her life and make the "seeking" and "reacting" very specific to her.

Your heroine might hate her life and want change, fall into change by accident, or want to protect the status quo. She might need to recover from pain, from past trauma, so that she can move on and heal her scars. She might be frozen, and spend the whole script thawing. She might want to go on an amazing quest, solve a riddle, or seek vengeance. She might want to be or do something extremely bad, but the guilt is eating her up.

Your protagonist needs to resolve the Heroine's dilemmas, sometimes to be able to access her inner Hero, the side of herself that is ego-driven, selfish, and identifies separately to others. Hero and Heroine are flipsides of the same coin. We need to be self-oriented and outwardly directed, and we need to be a human with the need for connection.

The main kinds of Heroine are the Outsider Heroine, Incomplete Heroine, Survivor Heroine, and Questing Heroine.

Outsider Heroines

These can be misfits, rebels, artists, lesbians, disabled women, older women, sick women, addicted women. Their dominant drive is to *seek life on their own terms, ones not defined by others.* It's ultimately not high on their agenda to belong to society, because they know on some level they won't, don't, or can't fit. Some Outsider Heroines have taken one look at the status quo and realized it's not for them. They don't want to belong; they are motivated to reject it, particularly if society labels them as somehow redundant or undesirable. They may be too unconventional in spirit. An Outsider Heroine is like a reverse fish-out-of-water. She's not sure she wants to go back in if it means losing a sense of herself. A Heroine might hate the judgments society makes about her through no fault of her own. Sometimes, the Heroine becomes an Outsider Heroine because she finally realizes she doesn't belong anymore, try as she might. She is never going to belong, so why fight it?

Sometimes she might be too poor, too ethnically different, too excluded by extreme poverty, age, or other inequalities. Sometimes a Heroine is an Outsider for something as simple as being a "woman returner," a woman who is going back to work after years of childrearing, plagued by lack of confidence. Sometimes she's an Outsider because someone's forced her there against her will.

Outsider Heroines don't often reintegrate into mainstream life if it means being untrue to themselves. Belonging in a healthy way requires healing, connection, and acceptance; an Outsider Heroine won't stop being an Outsider unless she is truly accepted by herself and others. Many women can relate to feeling "outside" due to equality still being a recent gain. Even high-achieving women feel they suffer "imposter" syndrome in their jobs, particularly when they're being successful due to the fact many male-driven environments have ways of being that feel alien to women. These women may feel they need to crush the Heroine inside them, and assume the Hero mantle to fit in. The woman who breastfeeds her baby in public and is asked to go to the ladies' room is momentarily an Outsider Heroine. By doing the most natural thing in the world, she can be rejected by others. Sometimes their journey is to discover they don't mind being alone if it means staying true to their values; other times it is about learning that they can belong if they find the right tribe.

Films and TV shows where the female protagonist identifies as an Outsider Heroine include: *The Good Wife*, *Bates Motel*, *Frances Ha*, *Blue Jasmine*, *Ricki and the Flash*, and *Saving Mr. Banks*.

Survivor Heroines

Victims, betrayed women, physically ill women, entrapped women, abused women, ex-addicted women are found in this category. Their dominant drive is to *seek a healthy life*: literally, to live. Sometimes life has dealt extra painful blows to a Survivor Heroine. She's been harshly knocked off center, and needs to find her balance. Needing to achieve closure on a major trauma can be a very powerful drive in a Survivor Heroine. Loss and bereavement after death are common to

Survivor Heroines when their whole identity has collapsed and they feel their world has ended after the loss they have suffered. Likewise, the deep scars of failed romantic love are very common. Infidelity, cruel rejection, being forced to give up one's true love, and the opposite, arranged marriage, are all frequent motivations for a Survivor Heroine to seek recovery from the past and a new life. Sometimes a Heroine seeks life in the face of ill health or death. Survival for these characters is trying to keep it together in the face of their own early death. The process of recovery from loss includes denial, despair, numbness, guilt, and anger, and Surviving Heroines experience all these emotions and more.

Survivor Heroines' stories tend to have powerful arcs where they start out in one state, and end the story in a much better situation, at least mentally. Persecution, violation, and brutality can leave these characters with deep scar tissue, so learning to trust and to accept help and healing may be a big part of their future paths. Sometimes there is no way of surviving a brutal regime that is designed to crush, and the chances for survival are slim. In the case of a kidnapper or crazy partner, that regime may be just one person.

Films and TV shows where the female protagonist identifies as a Survivor Heroine include: *Room*, *Maleficent*, *Big Eyes*, *Girlhood*, *Penny Dreadful*, *The Hunger Games*, *Game of Thrones*, and *Homeland*.

Incomplete Heroines

Rejected women, women yearning for love, women who do not feel emotionally whole, women with mental-health problems, and women who love too much are all Incomplete Heroines. The dominant drive of this Role-Choice is to *seek emotional fulfillment*.

Most romantic heroines fall into this category. These are women who seek balance in their relationships and need to work on their issues to heal their romantic problems. They often feel they need the love of another to feel whole, when really they need to learn to accept themselves. These women embark on very emotional and internal journeys to make sense of their relationships. They need to heal internal wounds that are getting in the way of either their own personal autonomy or their ability to find love.

The love interest of an Incomplete Heroine can often be her best healer and teacher, but sometimes he or she can represent her deepest pain. The importance of others and supportive relationships are usually critical to the healing of an Incomplete Heroine's loss of self. If there are problems in her relationships, it's often down to an unresolved problem or an internal wound that is crying out to be healed. The Incomplete Heroine has to face up to the fact that while life may have dealt her some blows, until she takes responsibility for her pain, she will not recover. A Survivor Heroine who has endured unbearable loss sometimes identifies with the Incomplete Heroine when she's achieved closure, but is left with feeling empty about life. It's like the desolation after the storm. Now that the actual trauma has taken place, the rebuilding needs to begin, often with the care of others.

Of all the different ways a character can identify with a Role-Choice, the Incomplete Heroine is probably the most frequent. We all have inadequacies, insecurities, hurts, emotional wounds, losses, hang-ups, and unfulfilled needs. We can compensate for inner emptiness in many ways. An Incomplete Heroine's problems tend to dominate her story. Meeting her inner need is vital to resolution of her story.

Films and TV shows where the female protagonist identifies as an Incomplete Heroine include: *The Good Wife*, *Big Eyes*,

Carol, Brooklyn, Philomena, Girls, Wild, Olive Kitteridge, Cake, Love, and *Mom.*

Questing Heroines

Leaders, saints, seekers of justice, police investigators and lawyers, warriors, and vengeance seekers and murderers are the most obvious types of Questing Heroines. Their external quest associates these female protagonists with the "masculine" Hero Role-Choice, *but the fact that they are female complicates the matter.* Why? Because the nature of their gender can often make them identify as Outsider Heroines as well. They might not be trusted or taken seriously by others because they are female. They might be unable to commit to the challenge themselves, reluctant to "lean in." Their quests can be creative, spiritual, and medical, anything where a tangible result can be achieved by effort and tenacity. The drive of these Questing Heroines is to *seek a result* in the outside world, and to deal with the obstacles or conflicts presented by their being female in a gender-divided world. Otherwise, they would simply be heroes. If the Questing Heroine doesn't solve the problem, there will be more deaths, more wars, more corruption, and more bad guys having their way.

Often Questing Heroines are monarchs, such as queens, who seek to retain power against insurmountable odds, perhaps to embark on quests to prove themselves as worthy. The loss of anything resembling a normal woman's life may lead them to feeling Incomplete, but the Quest is a dominant drive in them. Biopics are full of Questing Heroines who have to deal with gender baggage.

The morality of the Questing Heroine can often be a big question. Do her means justify her ends? Does she compromise or sacrifice her true nature to obtain her desired result? She may endure the whole conflict women frequently experience of being too many things to too many people. Can she meet the domestic and relationship needs of loved ones as well as the external task? Conventional notions of heroism can be upheld by the Questing Heroine, more so than any other Heroine Role-Choice, where "saving the self" comes before saving others. But even for the highest-minded heroines, there's usually a sting in the tail of heroism. If she succeeds in her quest, will she fail others who need her? Who or what does she sacrifice?

Your protagonist will relate to the Questing Heroine when she gives herself a mission. How she goes about achieving it will depend on her needs, her sense of identity, and the expectations on females in her world.

Films and TV shows where the female protagonist identifies as a Questing Heroine include: *Brave*, *Game of Thrones*, *Black Swan*, *Agent Carter*, *The Fall*, *The Honourable Woman*, *Scandal*, *Jessica Jones*, *House of Cards*, and *How to Get Away With Murder*.

The Role-Choice of Nurturer

Women "mother." It's what we are all trained to do, from day one. And "mothering" — loving, feeding, cleaning, tending, caring, and being totally alert and immediately responsive to the needs of others — is the essential job description for the Role-Choice of Nurturer. Out of all the Role-Choices, it has the most powerful influence over women's lives. The Role-Choice of Nurturer is when your protagonist puts another character or other characters' needs first, often at the expense of her own. As women are conditioned by culture to do this from the early years in their lives, this Role-Choice is often central to most female characters' sense of identity one way or another. It doesn't have to literally mean having children.

But this doesn't mean she's necessarily any good at it, or even enjoys it. Meeting one's own needs rather than other people's can be a big problem for your protagonist. How does she look after herself?

The Nurturer includes mothers, childcare workers, carers, nurses, or anyone whose role or motivation is to tend to the emotional and physical needs of others, even at the expense of their own. It can, of course, be seen in a male character. A female protagonist has to identify with the Role-Choice of Nurturer when she becomes a mother, cares for others, treats others' emotional wounds, or takes on an actual caregiver job. Nurturing can be pleasurable and satisfying for her, or the complete opposite. She might buck against the expectation to look after others, or she might take it in stride and accept it as one of her normal roles in life.

The different kinds of Nurturer are **Mother**, **Healer**, **Lover**, and **Sorority**.

Mother

The universal expectation for women to mother is exactly why *a protagonist who identifies as a mother tends to have a lot of her story time taken up with being a mother*. The kids literally stay in the picture! Her parenting is central to both the story and her characterization. Many female characters who are mothers find it a big challenge to define a sense of self beyond the Role-Choice of Mother! Becoming a mother is so powerful, it can completely change a woman's outlook and priorities. Researchers are always looking into why girls perform so well at school, outdoing the boys, yet are so unequally represented in positions of power in later life. Becoming a mother is a pretty obvious factor! Giving up work, reducing responsibilities, and having energy and brain space depleted or energized by the roles of caring and nurturing change women's abilities to "have it all." Whether you think that women are natural carers, or you believe that the expectations on mothers are another unfair division of gender roles, your attitude as writer is going to filter down into your characterization. Fathers can be the better "mother," better at hands-on nurturing, and this will also affect a male character's gender identity and how others relate to him. We are moving into an era where nurturing is equally divided between the sexes, and we see male characters doing plenty of identification with the "mother" Role-Choice. Do your male characters agonize about how to "have it all" and the demands of juggling?

Female protagonists who are mothers tend to be written for certain genres such as drama, thriller, and romcom. For the thriller, you might create a mother in jeopardy. The single mom who needs love might be suitable for a romcom or a dramedy. The mom who is doing her best to raise her kids but faces social problems is found in dramas and soaps. There aren't many action-thriller moms, in the same way there aren't many moms saving sons who have been kidnapped. Unless grandmothers are firmly acting and behaving according to type, writers seem even less inclined to choose them as protagonists. Reality TV is dominated by women who love being moms and wives, as it is part of their core identity. The male dad protagonist from a failed relationship can still have his children in the background, and he might pursue a story in which his kids are peripheral, but it's not as easy for his female counterpart to do the same. Unless her kids are grown up or elsewhere, she may still incur more disapproval for going about her external quests.

Women, for a whole variety of personal reasons, flee the family nest. Some never come back. There are many women who don't feel able to raise their children. Sometimes issues from childhood are reawakened when a mother has children, and these seriously undermine her capacity to care. Some women have full-scale psychotic breakdowns after birth, and never develop a deep bond with their child. Mothering, unsupported and isolated, can be harmful to a woman's mental health. To cope with mothering well, a woman (or man) needs emotional and practical support, and someone looking out for their needs. A tight-knit community or extended family might provide the care and support to your female and male characters who identify with the Mother Role-Choice. Then again, it might be the Nanny State in a utopian sci-fi!

Mothers who leave almost always cause big heartache; rare is the mother whose departure is treated as a peripheral story element. She doesn't have to be unlikable; maybe things just didn't work out, like Ricki in *Ricki and the Flash*. Maybe her ex was the better nurturer. Whatever the reason, it is still a huge deal for women to leave their children, so central to a woman's identity is the role of Nurturer.

Birthing in the West has been over-medicalized: a female character wearing a medical gown and lying back and screaming is a familiar acceptable cliché, as is the "ultrasound" moment when the parent(s) see the child for the first time. Perhaps there aren't many ways of making this a distinctive and original moment without being crass, but it's still a recent scientific phenomenon. Conception, abortion, pregnancy, and childbirth are very real experiences for many women, yet are processes prone to certain acceptable clichés and clichéd value judgments.

To have somebody completely dependent on you requires a total abnegation of your ego. Heroic quests are hampered when the leader is responsible for the total care of another human being. A woman's capacity to be a good mother can be idealized, normalized, or demonized. Every human being needs a nurturer, and those who mother others need it most. How do mothers — or men who mother — get their needs met? Many mothers have bad days, resent their children, and take stress out in fits of maternal meltdown. Some are never angry, or are too repressed to acknowledge their anger. Every person's experience is different, and everyone "mothers" in unique ways. The adaptation to the role of Mother is long and all-consuming; a parent's call to love and protect her children, and how she handles these impulses, will be unique to your character and her circumstances. It's a Role-Choice that will be strongly influenced by the SuperThemes at work in your characterization.

Female protagonists who reject the Role-Choice of the Mother reflect the reality that many women don't want kids. They may choose to nurture other aspects of their lives.

Films and TV shows where the female protagonist strongly identifies as a Mother include: *The Good Wife*, *Bates Motel*, *Admission*, *Homeland*, *Mildred Pierce*, *Mom*, and *Orange Is the New Black*.

Healer

Your female protagonist might identify as a Healer, tending to the physical and mental health of another character to bring about change and new life. It can be a job she has in the story (doctor, nurse, midwife, drug dealer) or simply a way of being that brings about a positive change in others. Healers tend to be people with a strong conviction to change others' lives for good, normally those who are vulnerable and unable to heal themselves. Healers understand they have a role and a duty, and they tend to make sacrifices so they can fulfill these roles and duties effectively. They basically believe they can do good and bring about a change in a sick person or system.

Female healers come from a noble lineage of persecuted women. For several hundreds of years, witches were burnt at the stake for offering alternative remedies that the establishment saw as subversive. The natural healthcare that is big business today has some of its roots in intolerance and fear. Your protagonist can't heal half-heartedly. It's a job that requires total dedication, but she could be reluctant about it. Sometimes healers ease the transition to death.

Healers can be wounded themselves, doing good to others because of either a gift, a talent, or a deep, empathic understanding borne out of their own experience of suffering. They can function as shamans, outsiders, or essential members of a community. Sometimes healing happens when the character is projecting their own need to be healed; sometimes it is better to take care of others than ourselves. Ask yourself: Who is healing your character, and why? Sometimes a character who heals has no interest in healing themselves, or healing others actually helps them heal in a private way. Healing can be a gender expectation of women in some cultures. Alternatively, many girls and women who want to pursue medical careers have faced numerous obstacles and resistance to their goals. You need to understand your own character's wounds deeply to work out who is best positioned in the story to help her recovery.

Your female protagonist might briefly stop to heal another during the course of her story. It could be a symbolic gesture of help to another that represents a change in your character, or foreshadows a greater turning point to come. Lovers, when all is going well, can heal each other through the power of their affection and the strength of their bond. Healing requires intervention and growth; in relationships, growth normally entails some kind of loss of identity and rebirth.

Films and TV shows where the female protagonist identifies with the Role-Choice of Healer include: *Nurse Jackie*, *Orange Is the New Black*, *Blue Jasmine*, *Wild*, *Cake*, *Bates Motel*, and *A Girl Walks Home Alone at Night*.

Sorority

The Sorority is shorthand for the huge variety of female collectives. The Role-Choice of Sorority is a regular feature in female-driven stories because it represents women's need to share, to empathize, to connect, and to feel understood by and with other females or "feminine" supportive men. How your character feels about the groups of other women in her life will be determined largely by how she feels about women in general.

Primarily, the Sorority Role-Choice is about sisterhood. Your character may experience conflict with her sister, or the opposite, intense love and loyalty. The rivalry, intense envy, and overt or covert hostility between sisters can be contradicted by a sense of unconditional, limitless connection. Your character can't choose a blood bond, but she can choose how she relates to her sister. Female sororities can explore these intense female "sisterly" dynamics in positive or negative ways.

A supportive sorority are the friends who pat your character on the back, listen to her woes, lick her wounds, and put her back on her feet. They allow her to bare her soul and not feel judged. They probably know her better than she knows herself. They are there for her, whatever time of the day or night. But female buddies don't always function as a bed of roses. Because they know your character so well, they can also give her a hard time. And like our family members, close friends can produce feelings of inadequacy or envy when we measure ourselves against them. Female friendships can be incredibly intense. How your character feels about her mother may influence her way of relating to other females. Having been raised by a cold mother may make your character unconsciously crave females, to heal the split; it could also make her distrustful of other girls or women.

Female solidarity, whether in small groups or large-scale movements, can be threatening to "The Patriarchy," forcing them to change their way of being to accommodate and power-share. Your male or negatively "masculine" characters might not be too happy about that, whether they are conscious of this or not. If you are creating a group of male characters, why choose only one token female character to be in the group? What would more females do to the energy? It might be the fact that your female character shuns Sororities and feels more comfortable in Fraternities. She simply might feel safer with one gender or the other. The token guy in a female Sorority is less commonly created by writers. Outsider Heroines who form sororities to make a difference to their own or other women's lives can be frowned upon or meet hostility. A Sorority can be made up of men and women if it embodies "feminine" qualities of solidarity, compassion, and care for others. Workers' unions have a Sorority energy in this respect; non-hierarchical management structures likewise.

Women-led organizations that serve to support women, women's political groups that serve to advance equality in law for women, and women's church groups are all forms of institutional sorority. Girls' schools are Educational Sororities. An Enforced Sorority can be institutional (e.g., prisons, the army), religious, criminal, or educational; the character could be stuck with other females as an expectation of others or due to her own election. But once in, she may find it difficult to adjust to the regime or find a way out. Alternatively, she might discover new ways of relating to women.

Films and TV shows where the female protagonist identifies with a Sorority include: *Suffragette, Orange Is the New Black,*

Girls, *Nurse Jackie*, *Girlhood*, *Maleficent*, *The Good Wife*, *Black Swan*, *Blue Jasmine*, and *Pride*. *The Real Housewives of Beverly Hills* depicts real sororities, with emphases on dynamics, glamour, wealth, and male and female dynamics.

The Role-Choice of Dependent

Some female characters are dependent on others, or they choose this way of being. Others are literally at the mercy of others and have no other choice. And then there are those who, to fulfill a deep psychological need to be looked after by others, convince themselves that they are helpless. It represents the part of human existence that is subject to or depends on the power, attention, or control of others. It symbolizes our vulnerability and our need for protection.

The Role-Choices of Dependent are **Child**, **Victim**, and **Lover**.

Child

Some female protagonists are children in terms of age, and by their very status are dependent on the care of others. Children have no power in many cultures, and therefore little responsibility. But they should have rights. Reflect to what extent the principles of the United Nations Convention on the Rights of the Child are reflected in your child characters' lives.

Maturity is all about becoming responsible for yourself, and others who depend on you. It's the circle of life. However, to what extent your character can retain the joyful exuberance of playing, having fun, being creative, and other childish capacities is something to consider when developing a female character. It can often be the case that we give more childlike fun and naughty antics to male characters.

Many female characters have had their childhoods stolen from them, having to grow up too fast, too soon. They may be child brides, raped, or put to work. Or they had a childlike parent for whom they had to take too much responsibility and who may have deprived them of childhood fun and play, intentionally or otherwise.

Some adult characters reflect the Role-Choice of Child because they don't want to grow up. They might be happy with having the power, but they certainly don't want any responsibility. While they can be old for their years, their development may have been arrested prior to adulthood by their attempts to permanently recapture a lost youth. The character that is a child at heart indicates an ability or need to make others care for them, or just let them be. This could actually be a strength — to a point, if it isn't too one-way for an adult relationship. Free-spirited female characters who are always chasing rainbows can be highly charismatic, with plenty of M-Factor. Retaining a childlike ability to explore, this kind of character recognizes no limits and has an endless sense of wonder, fun, and playfulness. If your character has these gifts, her freedom can be exhilarating not only for her, but also the audience. We might see the world through her eyes and relish in it. Maybe we don't want her to be crushed by harsh reality or the system.

Films and TV shows where the female protagonist identifies with the Role-Choice of Child include: *Girls, Girlhood, Some Girls, Frances Ha, Wild, Saving Mr. Banks,* and *The Good Wife.*

Victim

If your female protagonist identifies with the Role-Choice of Victim it will be because she is — or feels she is — at the mercy of another person's power, or because a social system has power over her, or a combination thereof. Alternatively, she could be identifying as a Victim in order to manipulate another person to look after her by "playing the victim."

Being victim of another's control is central to drama and a fundamental source of conflict. Sartre's "Hell is other people" nicely sums up the problems that we can find ourselves facing when we feel completely powerless. Victimhood is not a state most characters are likely to choose for themselves, but it is one we as their creators most frequently put them in. Women can suffer physical or sexual victimization due to male aggression. As more dimensional and powerful female characters appear on screen, female violence is also becoming a lot more common. Violence against the self, i.e., self-harming, can also be a form of victimization for which empowerment and healing are the only answers.

Often, feeling victimized can be a state of mind, and the only person who can help a character out of the negative mindset is herself. Women, just like men, need to empower themselves to feel in control of their own lives. A deep fear of failure or lack of confidence can prevent some female characters from actualizing their dreams. By convincing themselves that life is against them, they can avoid taking responsibility. Other victims habitually live in the blaming mode. If your character makes everybody else responsible for her terrible life, then she won't have to look within.

Many female-driven stories show a transformation in the main character, emerging from victimhood to an empowered state of being where she can take responsibility for herself and her needs. Empowerment is tremendously satisfying for the audience, as it gives us hope for self-determination. Try to work out to what extent your character might collude with being a victim, and the reasons she's doing so, in the backstory. Remember, your female protagonist will always be more memorable if she saves herself and others. Female characters are equally competent as saviors as their male counterparts just as they are in real life!

Films and TV shows where the female protagonist identifies with the Role-Choice of Victim include: *Maleficent, Wild, Girlhood, Game of Thrones,* and *Bridesmaids.*

Lover

If your female protagonist is devoted to love — wanting it, finding it, keeping it — it tends to be a big part of her story and this means she will identify with the Lover Role-Choice. We can still associate female characters with the ones who strongly need love, and female audiences with the ones who want to watch love stories. To what extent you want to downplay or "big up" love in your female protagonist's life will be shaped by your own attitudes toward love and romance, and the underlying reasons why you are choosing a female protagonist, but it is often hard to find a female-driven story where love doesn't have a central role. Love can be a double-edged sword. We let people in, but then we are vulnerable lest they hurt us. We keep people out; we are lonely and don't thrive. Or so the big romances lead us to believe. If there is a big love dimension to the story, how you feel about love and romance and what you want to say about it will play out in the characterization of your female protagonist.

When she identifies as a Lover, your female protagonist can make sacrifices, withstand long absences, and permanently give up her family. Love may make her a healer, a catalyst, and a revolutionary all in one. It could permanently change her life, even if it has to end. If a female character loves or needs love, to the point that "the other" is her whole universe, this tends to be the engine behind her whole story. She defines herself as a Lover, someone who can only feel whole if she is with the object of her affections, and if her loved one is equally committed. Of course, the fact that her love is requited could be an entire fantasy; she might have a girlish crush, or a powerful obsession.

Lovers can be doomed, destructive, or dark. If doomed, you might be interested in the obstacles that threaten and ultimately destroy your character. These can be external, the stuff of timeless, classic romances, such as when two soulmates are tragically parted through war, family, or cultural obstacles. Or one character falls out of love with another because their circumstances or feelings simply change. Maybe the other person gets ill, grows old, loses money, moves on. Fun-loving narcissists can dance off into pastures new rather than endure a period of hell. "I didn't sign up for this" is the classic defense for bailing out of a relationship when the going gets too tough. Tests of love often demand that the Lover examine her own contribution to the problem. Perhaps it is her selfish needs getting in the way. Perhaps she plays the victim, or perhaps her partner victimizes her.

We can frequently generate enough obstacles to love in our own mind; these are the self-destructive aspects of love. Your character or her partner might be too needy, too jealous, and too insecure, or too controlling, too manipulative, and too dangerous. She may be caught up in a self-destructive relationship, playing out unresolved patterns. She might not be able to do without love, somebody who invests too much and is always hurt or who has a fragile sense of self. She might hate the idea of being alone, but she might need a lot of healing to handle a functional relationship.

Loss of love can also be associated with Victim and Healer Role-Choices, where the character has to come to terms with who she is at the end of love. Divorce, death, and betrayal can all inflict huge emotional wounds that need time to heal. Breakups can unleash a new lease on life, or deprive a character of any sense of future. The character may wise up and see who was right for her all along when she's worked on her self-esteem issues. Or she can become vengeful, raging, and unbalanced in her quest to hurt the person who hurt her.

Amazonian love — where two idealists fall in love — can be electric and creative, but not particularly stable. These couples are a potent force for change, and if they become disillusioned by each other, it's because they think the other is selling out the shared dream. Infidelity can even be borne so long as their loved one still has their ideals in place.

Diversity in sex and love is finally increasing on our screens, away from heterosexual norms. Lesbian, gay, and trans romances are being written and produced, replacing boy-meets-girl versions of romance. There's a real focus on the complex nature of love rather than the one-size-fits-all "happily ever after" scenario. What happens after getting together can be as interesting as getting together, or the periods between being together. What aspects of love do you want to explore through your character? What are your romantic values?

Films and TV shows where the female protagonist identifies with the Role-Choice of Lover include: *Bridesmaids*, *Carol*, *Spy*, *Before Midnight*, *The Age of Adaline*, *Maleficent*, *Phoenix*, *Girls*, *Love*, and *Orange Is the New Black*.

The Role-Choice of Believer

Whether it is ideas, revolution, or religion, female protagonists who reflect the Role-Choice of Believer have a cause. Sometimes their convictions serve selfish reasons, but more often than not these are altruistic individuals who want to better the cause of man and womankind. These are women who have made this Role-Choice because they are ideological beings at heart. They want to improve the world and make it a better place. They can handle necessary sacrifices for their cause, and they aren't scared of conflicts, obstacles, or difficulties. They can be driven and workaholic, and go about life quietly or with a bang.

The Role-Choices of Believer are **Amazon**, **Rival**, and **Caryatid**.

Amazon

Believer characters who fight for the causes of equality and liberty as heroines are Amazons. These women are all about taking a stand for their cause, even if the cause is to live life as women on their terms. Making this type of Believer Role-Choice usually indicates your protagonist is angry or fired up about some kind of injustice or oppression. She could take a stand for herself, or on behalf of others, such as her family, other women, or another vulnerable group. Amazons tend to be galvanizers who want social change and are prepared to fight for it. Usually family commitments are second to her priority of protesting. Women wouldn't have the vote if some pioneers hadn't abandoned their familial lives to fight for suffrage. If there's one adjective to describe an Amazonian female protagonist, it is "empowered."

Sometimes Amazons have to be Outsider Heroines as well because the world isn't willing to accept their vision. They can be artists, writers, teachers, creatives of all kinds. Many Amazons are acutely aware of injustice against women or other vulnerable groups.

Sometimes contemporary Amazons are compensating for an inadequacy they perceived in their family. They might be motivated to become almost invincible as they go from success to success in the outside world. This can lead them to being unable to express vulnerability, or becoming overstressed from having too many balls in the air. But the high-achieving man who is driven tends not to be judged on his inability to be vulnerable. He is generally admired and his endeavors in the world praised, despite the toll. "They have taken too much on" tends to be used about women more than men.

A true Amazon knows that her ideals come first. She is a liberator, motivated to break down and transform hierarchies that oppress and feed off victims. She won't be scared to take a stand. A character can become an Amazon by chance. Her eyes can slowly be opened to injustice by being plunged into an oppressive situation. She might be the unlikely spokeswoman who discovers her strength as leader.

Films and TV shows where the female protagonist identifies with the Role-Choice of Amazon include: *Game of Thrones*, *The Hunger Games*, *Suffragette*, *Made in Dagenham*, *A Girl Walks Home Alone at Night*, *Maleficent*, and *Dear White People*.

Rival

Your female protagonist might set herself up as a Rival to someone else in her story. She might consciously pitch herself against another to prove herself. The Role-Choice of Rival is a galvanizing decision, one that can fuel or reveal her deepest insecurities. Being rivalrous is part of being human, and it all starts in the family. We are all rivalrous for love, for attention, for praise, for being special — all to fulfill the needs of our Egos. When it comes to writing your female character, pay attention to how you develop her as a Rival to avoid acceptable clichés, which can abound with female Rivals. The catfight is the old familiar scenario of two women at each other's throats (metaphorically or otherwise) for the love of the same man.

The wife-and-mistress rivalry, wherein the duplicitous man cannot make a choice between two women, is rarely seen reversed with a duplicitous female protagonist.

Your female protagonist might be consumed by rivalrous feelings for her sister. Older sisters frequently resent their younger sisters for having it easier, and younger sisters might resent their big sisters for being able to do more in general. If they're in her backstory, unresolved emotions might shape the way your female character relates to other women. She may resent her partner for being the favorite of one of their kids.

Women's rivalry in the workplace, where they compete to get a job done well, to win a contract or court case, should not only pit woman against woman. Women go up against men all the time in real life and win. Sports aside, women's competitive spirits are worthy of exploring in the world of work. Ask how your character identifies with winning, with being the best, with having more money and more success than people she works with or lives with. Does this make her undesirable? Do you believe that women are less attractive as go-getting winners? Is the quest-oriented heroine less attractive than her male counterpart? Is she going to be punished if she doesn't show solidarity and equality but instead carries on like a "me-first" go-getter?

Films and TV shows where the female protagonist identifies with the Role-Choice of Rival include: *The Good Wife*, *Orange Is the New Black*, *Brave*, *Mom*, *Frances Ha*, and *The Kids Are All Right*.

Caryatid

A Caryatid is a type of column, in the form of a woman, found in the temples of Ancient Greece. It's a good term for the female protagonist, who is the institution builder of her world, a woman who supports and maintains the status quo. Characters who identify as Caryatids need the system and they love the Establishment; they want to do their bit to uphold it. They thrive on social order, tradition, and hierarchy. You see the Caryatid in your character when she's eagerly trying to prove herself on the job, being a loyal wife, running her own business, and generally doing her bit for the good of the community in a way that doesn't rock the boat. Some Caryatids come in the form of the "Community Pillar," a woman who supports the local community without actively wanting to be in charge. Again, these female characters are most at home doing good in the community, knowing everyone well, keeping an eye out, and helping and lending a hand if things go wrong.

She wants solid foundations and tradition, with the quiet conviction that it's just the right approach. She's a safe pair of hands, generally respected and relied on by others to step up when needed. This doesn't mean she doesn't fight to conserve or preserve, but her battles will be through established or legal means if necessary.

Being or becoming a wife leads your character into the institution of marriage, where she is required to uphold her wifely duties according to culture and law. In this respect, becoming a wife for your heroine is like entering a Caryatid institution, even if she is more of an Amazon at heart. Lots of feminists get married and discover new sides to themselves, which can be confusing for them. Therefore some female-driven stories revolve around a character getting out of a marriage gone wrong, or leaving a marriage that she was forced into or that oppresses her. Your protagonist might be thought of as a bad wife, blamed for the breakdown of her marriage for failing in her wifely duties.

Happily married protagonists who are wives tend to have made a pledge of commitment entirely based on love, devotion, and providing a stable base for the family. Marriage in this sense is a sign of maturity and functionality, a role that many women use to forge a life-lasting bond with their beloved. Such a Caryatid will aim to take her marriage vows very seriously. If she's a Nurturing type too, then she'll be the perfect wife and mother, as far as society goes. Royal and aristocratic heroines are women who are expected to play their part in society in a Caryatid-like manner, or else run afoul of the nation. They are literally married to their royal duties.

A Caryatid may also come in the form of a female boss, a woman who chooses to lead, to control, and to compete. Bosses get a kick out of power and profit, whether it's real or symbolic. Female bosses want to achieve, and the domestic sphere is not likely to be their favorite place. Their natural habitat is the institution; their identity is largely professional. Bosses can show "feminine" intuition in doing their jobs well, but retaining power and doing the job is really the name of the game for these women. These women's internal conflicts are kept firmly under control. They are true Caryatids who are motivated to support the institution, but most important to them is maintaining their own role and status within it.

Films and TV shows where the female protagonist identifies with the Role-Choice of Caryatid include: *The Good Wife*, *The Iron Lady*, *Saving Mr. Banks*, *Call the Midwife*, *Veep*, *Madam Secretary*, *Homeland*, and *Game of Thrones*.

Masculine Role-Choices

The diagram below sets out the kinds of Role-Choices that are frequently associated with masculinity and male characters. There is a brief description of each masculine Role-Choice, with suggested conventional values attached to each. As traditional gender roles disappear from our lives, likewise in our stories both masculine and feminine Role-Choices can be seen in many characters, male and female. Try to work out which of these are evident a) in your female characters; and b) in your male characters. Remember the preferred SuperTheme of your story. Would it help if your female protagonist overtly identified with some of the more "masculine" Role-Choices? What effect would this have on your message? Consider switching them between the genders and how you would go about this.

Father

Provider, disciplinarian, head of the family household. Power and authority are frequently associated with the Father. The line of the Father is a core element of patriarchal systems such as inheritance, marriage, and hierarchical organizations and groups. Women and children identify through the Father's surname. "Mr." is the main title for men, yet women are still often asked to classify themselves as Miss or Mrs., as if the marital status of a woman should define her. The Caryatid within your female protagonist has no problem with the symbolic requirements and systems of the Father. Wealth and resources are passed down the line through the sons, normally favoring the eldest. The Amazon may be angry about this. The Father might have Amazonian energies, wanting his daughter to be free, to have every opportunity a son would. The actual "male" Father can be the better "mother," and have a closer relationship to your female protagonist. Being Mother may open up identity issues for him. He may also be the harbinger of social change, becoming a role model to other men as a way to reject aggression and violence. Your female protagonist may associate nurturing with the Father, as mentioned previously. When single parents run their own homes, they need to cover the functions of Mother and Father.

Fraternity

This Role-Choice represents informal or formal notions of brotherhood, the core of male bonding, that often reflect implicit and explicit rules and regulations of "The Patriarch." Honor, nobility, sacrifice, and other traditionally heroic values are frequently associated with brotherhood. Some female protagonists enter a Fraternity as fishes out of water, or they may seek to identify with the male brotherhood, preferring it to female Sororities. Non-hierarchical Fraternities can take the form of new men's movements with lots of caring Sorority attributes.

Rebel

This Role-Choice reflects the Outsider male or female who doesn't fit in and who seeks to subvert or reject authority. Danger and risk are frequently associated with the Rebel. Their motive is to live life on their terms, and to stick two fingers up wherever possible. They are frequently identified with the Child Role-Choice. Rebels can be relied upon for their energy and irreverence, rather than their commitment or steadfastness, unless their journey is about becoming mature and responsible. If you are writing a rebel, ask yourself if you allow your male rebel to get away with more than you would your female rebel.

Boss

This Role-Choice represents the head of the institution, normally the one who holds ultimate power. Power, control, and hierarchy are frequently associated with the Boss. It stems from the masculine version of the alpha male at the top of the hierarchy. The Boss is defender of the line, head of the tribe or clan, the king, the president, the male who has the last word and whose power is revered and treated as law. Boss describes the desire for power over others, the need to be top dog, a tough guy, as well as the need for groups to seek out a leader. Male power is so ingrained and customary that it's very pervasive in modern storytelling. The Boss Role-Choice can, in particular, be vulnerable to the sexual double standard in character development. For instance, you might let your male Boss characters be more respected and loved than your female versions. Female characters can be bosses with very different managerial styles. To what extent does your protagonist run an operation with hierarchical ("masculine") or inclusive ("feminine") values? How does she gain and hold power? Likewise, if she is subordinate, an underling without power, how does your female character relate to male bosses? Is she naturally rebellious, or does she admire men in charge? Is she talented, but can't break through the glass ceiling due to sexist practices and attitudes in the workplace? Or is she a "horrible boss"? Do her underlings not respect her?

Warrior

The Warrior Role-Choice can be the fighter who will serve and protect with might and force when commanded, or when the call to arms is more internal, because values or the safety of loved ones is under threat. The Warrior can be lawless, like the violent gangster or a Mafioso who kills for monetary gain, vengeance, or to assert power. Death and sacrifice are frequently associated with the Warrior Role-Choice, the aspect of identity that uses force to get results. A bunch of Warriors can turn vigilante and form gangs and even whole armies. Female Warriors can be as fearless, noble, and self-sacrificing as male warriors. They can be kickass and dangerous. Female characters relating to the masculine Warrior come in all forms, from proud mothers or wives to those who are disapproving, envious, or resentful of the male ability to fight. They also might identify with the Amazon Role-Choice, like the Suffragette "armies." Alternatively, they might be soldiers in armies, desperate to fight alongside their male brethren at the front line.

Child (Son)

The Son can be seen as the child apprentice to the Father/ Brother Role-Choices. The Son is the child's experience learning to be a Hero, first identifying with masculine values and roles. Discipline and responsibility are frequently associated with the Child/Son. He carries on the name, the line, so he is invested with privilege in many cultures. In many heroines' journeys, where the father is absent and the mother is somehow deficient, the eldest daughter may take on "oldest" son-like roles: providing for the family, supporting the mother, avenging the father.

Lover

The masculine Lover Role-Choice is in conventional terms the initiator of romance; he represents the wooer, rather than the wooed, in traditional roles. He (or she) may be creative and expressive. Pleasure, seduction, and sensuality are associated with the Lover. The female character may not buy into seduction or romance when offered by a male or female Lover. Conversely she may expect romance and feel disappointed by her suitor if he or she fails to deliver. The female seductress, who is firmly in control and single-minded in her amorous desire, is less common as a protagonist (possibly due to a pervasive fear of being a "slut").

Victim

The masculine Victim Role-Choice corresponds to the weak figure in Alpha Male "Patriarchy" who cannot defend or protect himself, either due to personal or institutional threats. He can suffer a loss of respect from his family or community. Showing fear humiliates him; because he cannot be a tough-guy Warrior, he is emasculated in the eyes of society. Weakness and helplessness are frequently associated with the masculine Victim. Your female character as Warrior may be inspired to protect weaker men; or she may symbolically castrate him in her identification as Boss who is threatened by men or just keen to maintain her power. Boy Victims of child sexual abuse are starting to appear on our screens, as in *Spotlight*. The reprehensible violation of the young and innocent by religious men, such as priests, is an abuse of the power of the Father.

Rival

The masculine Rival Role-Choice is caught up with winning and triumph, being the best, and pursuing wider recognition. Power and determination are frequently associated with the Rival. He or she is universally lauded for coming out on top. Competition is what s/he thrives on. If his or her means are fair, s/he is respected for going into the fight. Playing dirty is justifiable for Rivals with even less scrupulous antagonists. Your female character may detest, have mixed feelings about, or embrace masculine forms of competition that are based on only one person being the real winner.

⌁ EXERCISE ⌁
The Role-Choice Questionnaire

Imagine you are your female protagonist as she appears at the start of your story, and complete the questionnaire. By the end of the questionnaire, you will have developed the main Role-Choices with which she could be identifying. You should get a better sense of her identity and her relationship to the outside world, as well as her value system.

As you develop your story and your protagonist grows, develops, and confronts challenging situations, you will be able to see how her Role-Choices might change.

Role-Choice
⁓ QUESTIONNAIRE ⁓

1. What are your deepest beliefs? What do you stand for?
2. Who or what most influenced these beliefs and ideals?
3. If you have children, how would you describe your parenting style?
4. Who supports you? Do you support others? What does family mean to you?
5. What does beauty mean to your own identity? Describe your self-image.
6. What do you most love/hate about your job? What would you change about it?
7. If you don't work, why not? How do you support yourself?
8. What are your personal ambitions?
9. What are your career ambitions?
10. How far have you come in achieving them?
11. Describe your position in your community. Do you like your community?
12. How would you like to be remembered?

ROLE-CHOICES CASE STUDY:
Game of Thrones Female Characters

Game of Thrones depicts a brutal, tribal, patriarchal world where white family clans, "Houses," perpetually war for power. Add mythical beings and creatures into the mix! Violence, torture, sexual slavery, and general cruelty are the means that justify the ends when maintaining or achieving power. The female characters are at first identified as daughters, wives, and mothers who on the whole accept their place, until trauma, violation, loss, and regime changes turn their lives and often their value systems upside down. Older women and black women have little visibility or power in this world. Survival in a power-obsessed, clannish world depends on allies, strength, and information. Early in the series there are very few supportive or feminist sororities who represent a challenge to the patriarchal system of the family Houses. Females are motivated by power, but normally use it to preserve their lineage rather than enact social change. However, the Wildling tribes enable women to fight as Warriors and these females are able to have sex on their own terms. Targaryen Daenerys ultimately offers the potential to lead others toward a new world where equality, freedom, and peace can replace tyranny.

Arya identifies as a Child (Son) who witnesses the unthinkable when her family's power crumbles and her father is decapitated. Lost and alone, Arya becomes an Outsider Hero, someone who has to find her own way back to her family, only to witness the massacre of the majority of her relatives. Unlike Sansa, Arya is tough and rebellious. She also identifies with the Survivor Role-Choice, someone who won't give up and will do what she can by learning to fight to protect herself. Here she identifies with the Warrior. Arya doesn't identify as a Victim, as she has a naturally defiant fighting spirit. When she is blinded by her captor, this spirit is temporarily crushed, and she has to learn to survive once more.

Sansa Stark at first identifies with the Child Role-Choice, for she is a vulnerable, innocent, and dependent girl who needs others' protection. She doesn't appear to have an inner strength or strong moral compass. She is prone to being a Victim due to her lack of courage, and helplessly depends on those who offer her help without sufficient distrust. She is naïve and fragile. Sansa frequently finds herself a pawn that is traded, identifying as a weak Wife without any ability to fight back, escape, or control her destiny. She is an Incomplete Heroine who needs others to help her. She is a willing

Caryatid, wanting to maintain the social order through a good marriage, but also to protect herself. However, horrific experiences as a wife of the Lannister King open her eyes. Sansa's experience of being an Outsider triggers her development into a stronger, independent woman who is capable of knowing her own mind and trusting her own judgment. She is finally willing and able to defend the House of Stark as a leader, revealing identification with the Caryatid Boss.

Lady Stark, mother of Sansa and Arya, is a true Caryatid who upholds her noble duties and is a loyal and noble wife. At first identified strongly with the Mother Role-Choice, Lady Stark has to identify as the Father and Boss after her husband's death. She wishes no more than to protect her family's lineage, wealth, and power, and to protect her children. Ultimately she is a Victim, and brutally murdered, in spite of her attempt to fight to the end to save her children and the Stark line.

The Red Woman is a true Outsider and Healer, a witch with magical powers whose agenda and allegiances are shifting and destructive. She loses faith in both herself, her powers, and the new gods she worships when her prophecies do not come to pass. Her magic or "god" restores life to Jon Snow, however, reigniting awe in her abilities.

Daenerys starts out a helpless innocent Child, Victim, and Outsider Heroine of a doomed family line, the House of Targaryen, but ends up a Questing Hero, Heroine, Amazon, and Boss, champion of freedom, respect, and equality. She is the only character who stands firmly against the patriarchal system, but her own attempts to achieve change are constantly threatened and undermined by the reality of the universe and the seemingly entrenched values of violent power. She is often at the mercy of hostile entrapment, but doesn't identify as a Victim for long. She identifies as a vulnerable Lover and trapped Wife when she is made Khaleesi, wife of Drogo. However, she grows to love him. She identifies as a protective and devoted Mother to her beloved dragons. Using their strength and her awesome powers, she becomes a fearless Warrior.

Cersei Lannister identifies as a staunch Caryatid, Mother, and Wife who is a cold, calculating, and cruel killer. She believes in nobility, in privilege, in power, and in birth right. Unlike Lady Stark, Cersei is vengeful and sadistic, a backseat driver of the Lannister power. Blindly adoring of her children, she proves herself an overprotective mother with an unbreakable bond. However, she doesn't trust her children's abilities to think for themselves, and thus she treats them as political pawns for the good of the line. As a Lover, she is incestuous and without morality, bonded to her brother Jaime, the father of her children. She identifies with the masculine Role-Choices of Boss and Father when she gains power after her father's death in a hierarchical and callous way. When she is captured and shamed by the High Sparrow, having suffered a total loss of power, she is forced to identify with the Victim Role-Choice; this rattles her identity somewhat, but not for long. Cersei is ultimately motivated by the need for power, and only relates to others in terms of control and manipulation. She has to face the high price of her ruthlessness: loss of all her children.

Brienne of Tarth is a female knight who has pledged loyalty to Lady Stark to protect her children, ultimately including Sansa. Brienne has a soft spot for Jaime Lannister, who saves her from rape, identifying her with a hint from the Lover. As a fearless Warrior and questing Hero on a mission, Brienne doesn't identify as a Victim or anybody's Wife, and she will fight to the death if duty requires it. She forms a Fraternity with her squire. Brienne, being female, identifies as a true and noble Caryatid as she serves the patriarchal order, knowing her place in the hierarchy.

Margaery Tyrell is a skilled player and "professional" serial queen, using her charms to wield influence and marry well. With her grandmother Olenna, both women form a Caryatid Sorority from House Tyrell that buys into the patriarchal system of marrying for protection and strength. Marriage is a transaction. Feelings of love, except for her brother and aunt, do not come into it.

Obara, Nymeria, and Tyene are a fearless and violent Sorority from Dorne who are vengeful and fearless warriors; they relish the fight and kill for pleasure. Effective as a team, they use their powers of seduction to trap their prey.

Gilly is a wildling in love with Samwell Tarly, who protected her when she was vulnerable and a Victim. He took on her son as his own. Gilly identifies as a good Wife and Mother: loyal, dedicated, and brave. Gilly is also noble, someone who will do the right thing for those she loves.

Yara is a princess from the Iron Islands. She is a fearless Warrior who loves to fight and make merry as much as any male. She commands respect from men. She is attracted to, and sleeps with, women. As ruler of the Iron Islands, Yara identifies as Caryatid and Amazonian Boss when she forms a truce with Daenerys.

CHAPTER 4

The Real Heroine's Journey

We all relate to our characters in shifting, nebulous, and multiple ways. We choose to write certain characters who may mirror our experiences, our desires, our fascinations, our loves, our hates. Sometimes we choose them because we feel they are the best character to trigger laughter or sadness in others. We have emotional relationships with our characters borne out of a real care for who they are, what happens to them, what they want and need, and how they live and breathe in each moment. So we build and shape journeys that we hope will achieve all this and more. And playing a part in all of the above is an equally deep personal connection to the gender of our characters.

So am I automatically writing a Heroine's Journey, you might ask yourself, *if my protagonist is female?* Well, this depends on your definition of the term. At its most basic, "heroine" is the term you give your protagonist because she is female, and it's a conventional term for the female lead role; it is also the "feminine" equivalent of the "masculine" Hero. The Hero's Journey is a very well-known model put forward by Christopher Vogler in his book, *The Writer's Journey*. It's based on Jung and Campbell's anthropological studies, and uses the language of the heroic quest in a model of stages that can help you build the structure and arc of your main and secondary characters, be they male or female. Kim Hudson's book *The Virgin's Promise* (2010) provides a "gender neutral" Virgin who embodies both heroines' and heroes' journeys. Her model follows Virgin archetypes — again, for male and female characters — on their journeys to find their true selves (which are both masculine and feminine). Jungian Feminism has many models of archetypes and experiences that could be useful in helping you shape your female protagonist's journey.

In particular, Maureen Murdock's *The Heroine's Journey* (1990) is a useful model for emotional development, one she identified from being a Jungian psychotherapist working with many female clients. Murdock describes how women have to *"separate from the feminine"* (the safety of being mothered and nurtured) and *"identify with the masculine"* (the outside world) to find success in the outside world. But success can lead to a *"spiritual aridity"* (too many demands, feeling false and disconnected) and it is only by a *"descent to the Goddess"* that a person can come to a psychological healing stage of *"reconnecting with the feminine."* This enables them to *"heal the mother/daughter split"* (get in touch with their need to nurture and be nurtured) and also *"heal the wounded masculine"* (feel balanced with outer demands) so that she can become "whole." In this way, the heroine's journey is all about the self in connection with other people. To Murdock, both women and men suffer from living in a world where the "feminine" is denigrated, where healing, nurture, communion, showing vulnerability, feeling lost, and needing help are signs of weakness — and where success, status, hierarchy, strength, and ego-achievement are prized as masculine qualities.

A Heroine's Journey is one where the following are important "stages" — but like in life, these stages do not need to fall into any sequence if you use them in your story:

- Inclusivity and connection with others
- Nurturing, of self and others
- Loving, of self and others
- Intimacy and reciprocity with others
- Identity issues caused by expectations of self and others
- Vulnerability and breakdown requiring the care of self and others
- Lives go backward and forward, very rarely with forward momentum

Perhaps writers put female characters on journeys that have more of these "feminine" issues and preoccupations. Perhaps we can handle our male characters differently in how they show and express their emotional needs as we shape their journeys. Again, it is up to you to evaluate your work and the feedback you might get about how you are reflecting gender, and through which characters.

The bottom line is that all our characters have deeply emotional needs and individual gender identities, and everything from our own personal psychology up to the wider culture we live in shapes how we might show these on the page. And don't forget the role of creative impulse in our process! You could label more emotional "feminine" states and processes as *blue*, and "masculine" processes — like competing, fighting, winning, building, questing, et cetera — could be *pink*. Imagine your character's journey is a tapestry, and you weave blue for any of the feminine issues, and pink for the masculine. When you weave them all together on your character's journey, the journey isn't blue or pink, but instead looks very *lilac*! Maybe this is a little too simplistic, but you probably get the idea. *Star Wars VII: The Force Awakens* now has a noble, heroic, determined female protagonist! We take for granted that she is tough and strong. It might be really appealing to you as a writer to subvert the gender traits of your male, trans, or non-binary characters. This swapping, mixing up, and subversion of gender traits can be really fun, and useful in breaking down conventional stereotypes.

The Heroine's Journey in Male-Driven Stories

Extending the weaving analogy, the caring and compassionate side of men, and those moments in which they show complete emotional vulnerability (through a "descent," like a breakdown, or hitting rock bottom) could be called "heroine's journey" moments, or "blue" moments. We can see these stages in stories with male protagonists, and we don't typically label them "feminine," although it would be easy to. For instance, in *The Revenant*, set in a violent, male-dominated, ruthless world, the flashback structure enables wounded Heroine and Questing Hero Glass to enter other ways of being, to mentally commune with love and tenderness with his Native American wife and child; he lapses into these other states even when he is suffering extreme pain and cruelty. They heal and soothe him. The trees represent his communion with a peaceful, natural world, away from the machismo and destruction of the colonial invaders. Likewise, the character of Rust in *True Detective* has lost his identity and needs to heal after losing his daughter. He is emotionally empathic with women; at the end, his mask breaks, and he cries openly, needing the love and compassion of his partner Marty to help him heal. Both these moments of caring reflect integrated "masculine" and "feminine" sides of the characters. In *Transparent*, a father wants to identify as a woman. His transgender experiences and the impact on his family result in him — and them — identifying with both "masculine" and "feminine" aspects of identity.

As a writer you have a lot of freedom, and some might say responsibility, when creating your female protagonist's journeys. Remember your "WISE" might be playing itself out in how you are shaping all of your characters and the journeys they take.

Journeys of Emotional Identity

Inspired by Murdock's model, a "heroine's journey" in screenwriting can be one where you, the writer, want to strongly focus on a journey where your protagonist's sense of self in connection with others is paramount. It can also be a journey where her *identity* is under pressure and constantly compromised by having to relate to other people because of gender expectations. As the SuperThemes and Role-Choices suggest, "feminine" identity can mean many different things for a female character. For instance, a feminist in turn-of-the-century England would be attracted to the suffragette movement, and this could bring her into terrible conflict with those she loves (as in the film *Suffragette*). Her "Hero's Journey" is her outer quest to fight in the campaign, while her "Heroine's Journey" encompasses her identity issues as a person in relation to others. Just like the blue and pink strands, both journeys are completely intertwined.

As the roles that gender traditionally imposes on females in sex-divided societies can be very different than those imposed on males, they can take a different toll on a female's sense of identity. Sometimes this requires a female character to quell or crush her ego, give up on ambitions, or have problems on outward quests due to the perception and treatment of her by others; she might only want to care for others, or find this a real burden. Other times, feminine identity can mean joyous experiences celebrating being a woman and the ways that society may value this.

So in working out who they are on their Heroine's Journeys, your character is:

- *negotiating* who she is to both herself and others
- *reacting* to situations where gender might be an influential factor
- *feeling* emotions and *having* emotional needs, and expressing these

You need to know how your female protagonist will manage these processes at any given moment in a way that is both true to her sense of identity and that accurately reflects where she is on her Hero's and Heroine's Journey. To help you work this out, the following model of Phases could be useful. It's a model that aims to help you make connections between the *inner* emotional world of your heroine and *outer* gender-identity issues as she goes on her journey.

A phase is a moment or duration of time in the story when your heroine has emotional experiences that reveal or influence her sense of (gender) identity at any given moment

Phases are essentially an approach to building an emotional journey. Because they are related to your heroine's emotional identity, they ask you to consider how she is feeling at any given point or moment on her journey. When there are so many things to juggle in a scene, it can be easy to overlook where characters are in their personal journeys. Our emotions fluctuate from being very temporary to being longstanding states that can form an underlying frame of mind. These varying durations of emotion are exactly the same for your female protagonist! Using Phases may help you shape your female protagonist's emotional expression in a way that is unique to your character, as well as build complexity and a sense of identity. You will get to know her a little better as an individual: how she ticks, how she copes, how she functions. And how gender might be a factor in every situation of her emotional life, as it can be in our own.

Using a Phase Approach

Just as our emotional states go back and forward, and the way we feel about ourselves is constantly in flux, a Phase approach offers the writer fluid and flexible ways to think about emotional identity — from a specific moment in time to a much longer period in the story. Our ways of seeing ourselves are never fixed. In the same way, Phases may help you stream-line the ways your character relates to herself, to others, and to her station in life. They are not stages or progressive "beats," like in a journey model. The best way of describing them is the *substance of identity*.

It might help to think of a Phase like a phase of the moon, which transmits a different energy. In the same way, a Phase in your character's journey is a moment or duration of narrative time with a particular energy.

The Phases are truly flexible, and there's no prescriptive ways of using them. While the Phases are not readymade blueprints for structure, they do complement any screenplay format you are using — whether it's the classic linear structure, a "complex" linear structure (where the narrative unfolds in two or three different linear storylines), an arthouse nonlinear structure, or even a circular structure.

Imagine, just like the blue and pink strands of heroes' and heroines' journeys, the Phases are strands of many other, different colors of thread, like a rainbow. These colors can weave through your screenplay's tapestry; certain colors of thread will be stronger in certain sections, and weaker in others. There might be solid little slubs here and there where a Phase dominates. The colors might disappear for a while, only to come back later on. Some threads you can see in the background running evenly all the way through. Some of the Phases just might not feel right for your story. They might just work better as aids to help you develop the backstory of your heroine (all her life experience until the story begins).

Of course you can use them to help you structure your story by mapping which phases feel right for each act. But as you know and get to use them, you'll find that they become alive. So now let's take a look at them.

1. IDENTITY PHASES
   * **Transition**
   * **Maternal Lessons**
   * **Father Distance**
   * **Adornment**
2. RELATING PHASES
   * **Self-Regulation**
   * **Desire for Union**
   * **Loving Too Much**
   * **Retreat**
3. MOMENTUM PHASES
   * **Violation**
   * **Crossroads**
   * **Eruption**
   * **Path to Potential**

So now let's look at each group of Phases in more detail.

The Identity Phases

The Identity Phases reflect the moments in the story that are concerned with your heroine's *changing* identity. It's where she's dealing with her direction in life, the things getting in the way of finding herself, and the image she presents to herself and the world.

Transition

The Phase of Transition reflects your character's initiation of or response to change in her story. All characters, like all people, need some kind of change, even if this need is not consciously recognized by them. Changes can be chosen, enforced, or even coincidental. It can be brought on by one of women's many physical changes through life: menstruation, ovulation, pregnancy, birth, the menopause and aging processes. Your heroine may have walked out on a marriage, started a new job, decided to commit suicide or rob a bank. In your story, the Phase of Transition occurs when your character is in freefall, either having jumped or been pushed. It is the period of time when she endures the loss of the old and anticipates the new. It signifies a fundamental change of direction and a temporary loss of identity.

On a psychological level, your character may be ready for change, or totally unprepared for it. Or she could be somewhere in between the two, of two minds and hesitant. She may be feeling confident, vulnerable, or even terrified at the unknown quantity of the prospects ahead. In the Transition Phase, a heroine tends to be out of her depth, but there is absolutely no going back. There is a general feeling of release in this stage, like a leap of faith. She is on the verge of a new life that will change her in a way she can't yet know.

Your heroine may start her journey in Transition right at the beginning of your story. Alternatively, Transition might occur much further along in her journey, or even at the end. It can also reoccur several times during the course of your story at any point she has to move on and out.

Maternal Lessons

The Maternal Lessons Phase presents your character dealing with her values surrounding being a woman, and how she negotiates her "feminine" identity in contemporary culture. Every woman "deals" with being a woman every day of her life, whether this is conscious or unconscious. All women have feelings about being female — angry, happy, contented, frustrated, complicated; you name it, and your protagonist will have experienced it at some point in her life. She might not even be aware of some of the baggage she carries about her gender. She might be totally unconscious of a deep underlying rage toward men. She might completely identify with men and shun any conventional notions of femininity. She might live as a tomboy, butch lesbian, or transvestite.

Maternal Lessons also represent the mother/daughter relationship and to what extent, in the story, the mother/daughter relationship is bonded or broken. As women in Western culture do the lion's share of the child-rearing, the mother is normally a baby girl's first relationship. The mother looms large in her early life, an omnipotent force. She is a goddess-like being on which her daughter is completely dependent for survival. Some adult women feel they cannot ever achieve distance from their mother, no matter what they do. Where a boy can more easily separate from his mother because he has a male father and a masculine culture to welcome him, the girl has to accept that she will become like her mother, from whom she is trying to individuate. You can see this seemingly unbreakable bond well in mother/daughter relationships, even the bad ones.

Therefore a *mother* is most often a child's strongest and most powerful female role model, one who wittingly or unwittingly transmits powerful messages about femininity. These are the symbolic or literal "maternal lessons." Your female character lives those messages, either by rejecting them or identifying with them. Many women consciously try everything possible to not turn into their mothers! But if your protagonist has a close and loving relationship to her mother, it will be harder for her to resist identification with her mother's attitudes about gender, progressive or conservative. They could range from respect for men and male authority to resentment or distrust of men in general.

So how do Maternal Lessons function as a Phase in your story? They occur when the protagonist is dealing with her relationship with her mother (or the person who functioned as "Mother") and the messages that she learned from this relationship, positive or negative. Remember, the "dealing with" could be entirely symbolic. Your character could be playing out the Maternal Lessons she learned in any situation; it doesn't have to be with her mother. What if she didn't have a mother? Well, this is a Lesson in itself, all about loss of a female figure and how your protagonist is affected by it. Characters without mothers can frequently yearn for a deep sense of emotional nurturing and embrace.

Unhelpful Lessons that your heroine might believe can take these forms:

Women's lives are hard.
Women should be looked after by men.

Women should put their needs second and put others first.

Women rival each other for male attention.

Women shouldn't trust men.

You are turning into your mother.

Women have to be beautiful to get ahead.

Don't explore your body.

If you eat that, you'll get fat.

If you form a relationship with your father's new partner, you are being disloyal to me.

Women should stick together.

Keep young and beautiful.

While helpful Lessons can look like:

Women can lead happy and fulfilled lives as independent, unmarried, single women.

Women and men have equal rights.

Nothing and no one should hold you back from pursuing your dreams.

Women have a right to childcare.

I love you and will always be there for you.

A man can be as good a parent as a woman.

Women's aging processes are beautiful.

This is what you should understand about your body...

You have a right to say no.

Women have a right to earn the same as men.

How your character relates to Maternal Lessons could alter as she grows on her journey. She could gradually arrive at a point where these Lessons are challenged in some way by others, by situations, and/or by her own changing value system. She might abandon them, defend them, or at the very least have a major rethink. It often comes in the form of confrontations and/or healing relationships with real or actual mother figures.

This Phase will appear in your story when a female character is confronted with or acts out her internalized values about being a woman, whether she's doing it consciously or unconsciously. Parenting in a different style than the way she was parented can be a conscious choice made by your character. How she raises her own kids will say a lot about who she wants to be, and how successful she is in being this person.

Examples of Maternal Lessons in film and TV include: *Brave*, *Mom*, *Wadjda*, and *Bessie*.

Father Distance

The Phase of Father Distance is seen in those moments or periods of time in the story when your character has issues with men because of internalized or externalized messages about masculinity. A father is probably her first male role model; he forms and influences her attitude toward men and "the masculine." Your character may have a very positive role model in her father, and this can build an instinctive trust in men. Some characters may be unlucky, and have a negative father experience due to absence, abandonment, work, or estrangement. They could experience a mixed bag. It can be confusing when a character has Maternal Lessons that tell her men are bad in some way but she feels loyal and close to her father.

Father Distance can be seen as the degree of affinity your character has for the male sex. Your character may manifest extreme distance as insecurity, fear of abandonment, distrust or dislike of men, or a deep hunger for male attention. Your character may act out these emotions through: a need to seek approval from men; fear of, or anger with, men; low self-esteem; expressions of inner emptiness; fear of abandonment; or a fear that those who receive her care pose threats to her female identity. It may come out as a total rejection of men as sexual partners. Father Distance can be internalized through messages like:

No man will ever love you
Men can't be trusted
Men leave!
Men are selfish
You will accept that you will be judged and defined for your looks
You will not grow old, and if you do you will try to hide it for as long as possible
You will be the main carer of children
Men's work is more important
You will learn to put your own needs second
You will dread being called "slut" and modify your sexual behavior accordingly
You will feel inhibited about asking for what you really want in bed
The family comes before your career
If you want your marriage to work, you will put your career second
Don't put yourself first

It may be part of your character's journey to come to terms with how she is being held back by negative emotions toward men. Many women certainly feel they live life on their own terms today, with supportive and respectful men. But aspects of these Father Distance messages can still linger in families or the wider culture.

On the positive side, many heroines have zero to very short lengths of Father Distance because they have loving and close relationships with their fathers. If your protagonist has a father who provides nurturing warmth, intimacy, and care, then she will have very little Father Distance. In fact, you could say she receives positive Maternal Lessons from a male role model. She may have a solid foundation of self-esteem that has been validated by the love she had from both parents. For this female protagonist, negative Father Distance could only affect her in her external life; for instance, if there is a glass ceiling at work. She may not even perceive inequality between the sexes, as she has a high sense of self-regard as a woman. Positive Maternal Lessons and short Father Distance, in the family or wider community and culture, help girls become self-reliant, strong, and successful.

If her father is loving toward her, yet flawed in some way, Father Distance can be fraught with complex emotions for your protagonist. She may crave and idealize an impossible dream, or someone she loved and lost. She may be someone who prefers the company of men, a one-of-the-guys type. If she feels uncomfortable in her own body and with her own gender, she may become female-to-male trans, or identify as non-binary.

Father Distance is the principle behind the creation of every sensitive romantic hero, and every two-timing cheat. Sometimes, the Phase of Father Distance isn't very romantic after all. That's because it isn't about real love; it's about your heroine's unresolved projections about men. As a Phase in your heroine's story, Father Distance reflects a female character projecting her deepest feelings about men onto another character, usually male.

Self-limiting attitudes prevent your heroine from real emotional growth. Think of the characters that represent her internal conflicts and projections. Do you want her ideas about men to change over the course of the narrative, or do you want the male-dominated world to change for your heroine?

Remember both Maternal Lessons and Father Distance are metaphoric, and can be helpful as well as unhelpful. You don't have to give your character an actual mother or father in her story, but most of us have somebody in our lives (such as peers) who were important to our nurturing and care when we were young. If you character had nobody, then these lessons will come from the wider culture and community.

Examples of Father Distance in film and TV include: *Wadjda, Girlhood, Saving Mr. Banks,* and *Mom.*

Adornment

The Phase of Adornment concerns how your female protagonist relates to her own physical being and self-esteem issues. Every culture has different values and attitudes about beauty, and how females are expected to conform to ideals. In the West, it is very hard not to feel pressure to look good through staying slim, acting young, and being as attractive as possible. Clothes and accessories are indications of wealth and success. Not making an effort is seen as not doing your best, and indicates something about your status or self-esteem. The Phase of Adornment focuses on your female protagonist's feelings about her bodily image, and the relationship she has with her own physicality. When you imagine her, you will probably see her as a physical being. She will be a type, have a look. Her skin color, her age, her shape, her hair color, and more often than not, her level of attractiveness (which is all too often stated in screenplays after the female character is first introduced) are all choices you will make in your head. But it is up to you to consider how important, and why, you are making those decisions if you want others to know why these are important when they read your screenplay.

Consider what your story is saying about female beauty from a cultural point of view. Any statement you are making about it could originate in your female character's issues with her physical identity. Maybe you think it's most desirable for all women and men to look their best. The huge emphasis on youth, beauty, and size affects all women, and it will also affect your character one way or another. Very often, her attitude toward this aspect of your character's identity will come in the form of a Maternal Lesson that she will accept or reject. How much you acknowledge this in your story is up to you. Far more than a man ever will be, a woman is judged by her looks first and her brains second.

How can Adornment function as a phase in the story? How does your character relate to the pressure? What does looking attractive mean to her? How does being unattractive affect her self-esteem and shape her character? We often see female characters panicking about what to wear. Less so with male characters! This is the classic externalization of the desire to please. Pride and confidence in her looks, and the way she presents a mask to the outside world, are also very telling. Does she look like a slob until she dresses to go out?

What do appearances mean to her? If your character is asked how she would describe expectations about female body image, what would she say? Is she feminist, seeing misogyny and sexual double standards everywhere she looks? Is she ultra-feminine? Or does she consider herself to be normal? How does her attitude to body image compare to her mother's? Or is it a non-issue for her, as she has natural confidence and doesn't think about it that much?

Who were your character's first female role models? What did they teach her about body image and being a woman? Or about the color of her skin, or her body size? Is she physically able? How does she feel now, about herself, at this point in the story? Is this going to change? If your character is older, the Phase of Adornment might reflect her feelings of inadequacy or invisibility now that she is no longer a young woman; conversely, she may embrace her aging self with healthy self-love.

Examples of Adornment in film and TV include: *The DUFF*, *Girls*, *Black Swan*, *The Age of Adaline*, and *The Huntsman*.

The Relating Phases

The Relating Phases concern your character's actions, attitudes, needs, and emotions regarding her relationships. They show how other people influence her sense of identity, and the reasons behind her relationship choices.

Self-Regulation

The Phase of Self-Regulation reflects your protagonist repressing herself or holding herself back. It can take many forms, such as putting other people's needs second to her own, or denying herself for other, more complex reasons: danger, risk, conflict. It can be momentary and fleeting, or a lifelong condition.

A major part of feminine identity is the requirement for a woman to put her needs second to those she loves, as well as people she doesn't know so well. It can cause conflict with the self. With loved ones, the need to Self-Regulate usually occurs because women are conditioned to be nurturers, a Maternal Lesson that can be passed on from mother to daughter. In an ideal world, your character would be blessed with parents who help her build up a strong sense of identity so she can go for what she wants and not hold herself back out of fear of being judged. If she isn't, or if circumstances limit her opportunity, she might want something more for herself, something different. But it won't be easy for her.

The opposite of Self-Regulation is no regulation, losing all boundaries. The worst extreme is when things get out of control and the character places herself in a very self-destructive situation, or places others in danger. Addiction of any kind, left untreated, only ends up taking over the addict's functional self.

So how does Self-Regulation work as a Phase in your story? Essentially, they are the moments where your character is confronted with a choice to assert her own desires, or to restrain herself and do the right thing by or for others. A whole story can be based on a self-regulating character who needs to break out, or it can be a moment where the character holds herself back or throws caution to the wind. Your character might face a dilemma if her needs become a major problem for her male partner or for society. She might follow her will with abandon, or deny herself. It can play out in communication: a character might lose her voice or silence herself to avoid conflict with others. That's why female characters who don't conform, or speak their minds, or who want something different can be more harshly judged. This can manifest as being silenced, or as silencing herself. She may hold back, fearful of judgment and scared of being labeled a "difficult woman" or a "bad girl."

Try to work out how your character addresses women's expectation to Self-Regulate. Sometimes it is difficult for a character to balance her expectations with her need to be true to her personality. This can pose major internal conflicts for her, as she feels split between wanting to do things for herself and fearing being seen as selfish and unreliable. She may get used to others stepping forward and taking control. The world can seem like a frightening place for your character if she is being emotionally or physically abused.

Protagonists who need approval from other characters might fear being judged. This stems from a tendency in women to blame themselves for things going wrong, itself a by-product of being the Nurturer. She might feel her own behavior has brought a bad situation on herself; if she hadn't made certain decisions, this would never have happened. Taking too much responsibility for a situation shows a Regulated Self. This is a classic symptom of Self-Regulation, wherein your female character hasn't internalized positive Maternal Lessons that help her understand that she doesn't have to blame herself.

If Self-Regulation is seriously undermining your character, it can often be linked to the Phase of Eruption (see below). The Self-Regulating part of her at first tries to be nice, but then — enough, already! She erupts. She might explode and walk out. Eruption in the form of maternal meltdown is a very common way of women informing their families that they've had enough.

Your character may make odd choices regarding what's best for her own Ego, although in another light they might actually be good for her relationship. Or vice-versa: she's go-getting and needs to learn to self-regulate. Or those who love her want her to do more, but she holds herself back. Self-sabotage is complex, but is frequently seen in characters who have chronically low self-esteem or abandonment issues.

You might want your character to have high self-esteem and be extra alert to any issues that might make her put up and shut up. She doesn't care what people might call her; she's going to do things her way. She has self-respect and is assertive. She intends to play fair, and expects the world to do the same. Examples of Self-Regulation in film and TV are *Precious*, *Wadjda*, and *The Good Wife*.

Desire for Union

The Phase of Desire for Union reflects your protagonist's need for intimacy, love, and emotional support, whether platonic, romantic, sexual, requited or unrequited. This Phase is all about your protagonist's emotional, physical, human needs for connection with others. It is one of the strongest Phases in the vast majority of female protagonists' stories focusing on relationships and finding love. This is because of the Nurturing Role-Choice that women are conditioned to follow from a very young age, the Maternal Lessons and Father Distance issues that orient women to needing love and affirmation of love, and all the other cultural messages shaping women's lives. In this respect, it can last a whole story, or be momentary, depending on who your protagonist is, what she wants, how a "union" fits into her life during the story, and what society expects of her. A protagonist's self-esteem can be dependent on close and supportive relationships: friends, loving family members, lovers, and long-term partners. Alternatively, she may be a loner who only wants quick sex on her terms. She may have no need for supportive close relationships, as she finds they get in the way of her life goals.

As a shorter Phase, it can take the form of: a bad date; a one-night stand; chatting to a friendly stranger in the ladies' rest room; a girls' night out; or a glance across a crowded room. That fleeting but intense impulse to connect with another. The desire for the touch of another can reveal a lot about her state of mind.

Sometimes, when a character has been isolated and cut off from others due to trauma of some kind, a Desire for Union reflects that she is in the healing process. She isn't rejecting others; she is now able to reach out. Or others come to her, offering connection, and your character is now ready to accept love.

Your character may just stumble into the Phase by meeting someone unexpectedly, and before you know it, she's head over heels. Ambivalence can be an interesting dynamic in the Desire for Union Phase; the character is blowing hot and cold, unsure of her feelings. She might not be wanting the partner, or not wanting anyone else to have them.

Family scenes, showing the sense of belonging offered by the family unit, are very common in this Phase. It includes the craving for cozy and warm situations, the way of being that the Danish describe as "hygge." Your character may feel happy to be with her family. Loving friends can also symbolize a family group that the character relies on for validation and support. A wedding is a symbolic fulfillment of the Desire for Union, but a marriage is the ultimate test of the durability of that desire. The many tests of love during a marriage — children, stress, new partners, changes in the wider world, poverty — can seriously make each partner question where the love has gone. Tragic romances, where the beloved has gone or died, show an impossible Desire for Union that may completely overtake your character. Loss of a parent in early life may plague the adult character who does not feel whole.

Examples of Desire for Union in film and TV are *The Fault in Our Stars*, *Philomena*, *Bessie*, *The Best Exotic Marigold Hotel*, *Saving Mr. Banks*, *Wild*, *Maleficent*, and *Girls*.

Loving Too Much

Loving Too Much is the Phase in your story where your character's love of another has an overwhelming impact on her identity and decisions, so much so she loses sight of her own needs. This Phase is akin to Self-Regulation in that the protagonist experiences a total loss of identity and her grip on herself as she is driven by an obsessional need for love or sex, which can be largely negative depending on the context. It can be manifested in overprotective love, or an unhealthy desire. Whatever the cause, it reveals an internal imbalance in your character, who has to deal with the overriding emotions of desire and how they impact her life. Like any addiction, obsessional love and sex can ultimately be harmful.

Obsessional love can take many forms in a story: heartbreak, getting over someone, needing a boyfriend to fill some kind of internal vacuum or emptiness, or a monumental crush. It's when the character loses perspective because of love, and all her actions revolve around getting the loved one back into her life on her terms.

Abusive relationships are a big source of the Loving Too Much Phase, since the protagonist feels trapped by her own feelings. Normally, these kinds of characters have abysmally low self-esteem, and haven't yet healed sufficiently for a healthy kind of relationship. "Love" can be confused for co-dependency, or exist in a form of familiarity and need for security. It's the "better the devil you know" syndrome. The Phase of Loving Too Much forms the basis of a lot of the damaged character's story; she wrestles with her conflict regarding her significant other's unacceptable behavior. Should she leave? It can also be visible in the state of mind of the character who is looking for love and goes from relationship to relationship, always convinced the new partner is The One.

The Phase of Loving Too Much can make a female character take enormous risks for her significant other, literally putting her security or even her life on the line. She will sacrifice herself, even when the odds are against her.

Can your character love her children too much? Yes, when it stifles their development and becomes more about fulfilling her needs and anxieties, as opposed to theirs. Overprotective parents tend to have unresolved wounds from their own childhoods. They could have been emotionally or physically neglected. You can use this Phase in scenes and sequences where this problem is generating lots of conflict between parents and children.

Loving Too Much is a common Phase in female-driven stories where love heals all, as in the romance genre. Here, Loving Too Much is something to be celebrated, as is shows that dedication to the object of her affections pays off big time for the protagonist! Normally, some kind of internal growth is required of the protagonist before she receives her reward. Examples of Loving Too Much in Film and TV are: *The Five-Year Engagement*, *Big Eyes*, *An Education*, *Phoenix*, and *Orange Is the New Black*.

Retreat

Retreat is the Phase in your story where your heroine needs to hunker down into herself, and relate *only* to herself. She needs to be alone in the purest sense. When your character retreats, it is usually as a powerful reaction to change, trauma, loss, injury or sickness, grief, despair, mental-health issues, or a need for contemplation. Your character will need to withdraw from the world, from her friends or her lover, because she can only endure being alone. People can retreat to be themselves, and do things in private that are unacceptable to others or which they are ashamed of but which help them survive life. Self-mutilation is a very private act, as are binge-eating and bulimia. Retreat can be triggered by biological processes and changes such as menstruation, female genital mutilation, childbirth, menopause, and aging. Some cultures see menstruating women as unclean and require them to live separately.

Sometimes a character has had it with being defined by everybody else's needs, and she needs to go off into the symbolic wildness and find herself. Maybe she just wants to feel like herself, without all the pressures or roles she has to play in life. Fame is another extremely testing challenge. The famous female character may need or crave the Phase of

Retreat to keep in touch with her true self. In general, trying to be something for others, putting on a different mask hiding who and what she really is, can lead a character to snap and need to withdraw.

The bereavement process requires withdrawal from normal life, except when a character is actively in denial of her pain. The acute pain of losing a loved one is the hardest thing to bear. If it's her child, her lover, another close family member, or her best friend, your protagonist will feel it like a mortal wound.

Any form of incarceration against your character's will is an enforced retreat from ordinary life as she knows it. This Phase can happen in the backstory or the future. It may be prison, rehab, being held hostage, or being a displaced person. The Retreat can be scarring or fearful.

Retreat is a Phase that can be a scene or two long, last a sequence, or literally drive a huge part of the Story. The character's whole arc can explore her coming out of a Retreat.

Examples of Retreat in Film and TV are: *Clouds of Sils Maria, Phoenix, Cake, Wild,* and *Orange Is the New Black.*

The Momentum Phases

The Momentum Phase in your female protagonist's journey is the time when she has to take action due to external factors putting her under duress or forcing her to take control. It focuses on her need to make progress and transform her life. It occurs when she may be under pressure to act, or she is following a path of her own volition. It is the moment when her emotions are feeling galvanized that she makes a decision or takes an action, changes direction or consciously seeks out change. The Momentum Phases are the times of personal agency.

Violation

The Phase of Violation reflects your character's traumatic experience of being aggressed — or of being the aggressor. We are surrounded by violence on screen, and as female protagonists become more complex and darker, they are engaging in more violence. To what extent the Phase of Violation appears in your protagonist's journey will depend on her character, her culture, the level of threat she faces, and the means she has at her disposal to defend herself. It will also depend on the genre you are writing in, and your own value system. If as writers we associate female characters as Victims to masculine aggression, are we naïve? Certainly the popularity of increasingly violent female characters reflects an interest in, if not a hunger for, violence in audiences.

At some early point in a woman's life she comes to terms with the fact that she might not be able to defend herself from assault, violence, rape, or abuse. This realization might propel her to empower herself to deal with any aggression against her. Being violated or victimized is about feeling powerless, vulnerable, and no longer in control. It may be painful or life threatening. It can be psychologically destructive. Violation as a Phase symbolizes this threat to your protagonist, whether it's real or actual. She may only want to use her strength to do good, like a superhero. She may fear her own strength or lack of self-control.

The flipside of the Phase of Violation is perpetuation of aggression by the female protagonist. Consider how your character might be aggressive in word or action. Why is she like this? Is the society dangerous? Is she mentally ill or disturbed in some way? Was she born evil and destructive? Envy of other women able to bear children may lead to atrocious crimes by women. Women may take vengeance for sexual betrayal by becoming castrators. Vendettas, unjust law enforcement, unreasonable criminal penalties, and the primal desire for an eye for an eye are all factors that may drive your protagonist to violence.

Fear of rape or other sexual violation terrifies many female characters, ultimately transforming them into perpetuators. The message women sometimes grow up with is that they are responsible not only for their own sexual behavior, but their male partner's conduct as well. Whatever the cause of the violation, the character can feel wounded to the center of her being. If she remains in denial, it often becomes part of her journey to finally admit these feelings, and process her experiences.

Less common on screen is the violence that women inflict on themselves, such as self-mutilation and self-harming. Eating disorders offer ways for female characters to maintain a form of control.

Examples of Violation in film and TV include *Agent Carter*, *Game of Thrones*, *The Girl on the Train*, *The Hunger Games*, *Orange Is the New Black*, *Maleficent*, and *Hannibal*.

Crossroads

The Phase of Crossroads reflects the time when your heroine is presented with several options, each of which could take her life in a completely different direction. Every time we make a choice, evaluating our circumstances and different ways to go, we are experiencing Crossroads in our lives. *If I do this, this might happen. But if I do that instead, then maybe I will or won't get this.* Crossroads are Ego-driven dilemmas that reflect your protagonist's decision-making processes. They are very subjective, and clearly reveal your character's value system and her sense of identity. A decision made by a character under pressure is a staple of drama, but some Crossroads can be entirely affected by gender for many female characters. Major life choices include: how and when to have children (knowing that isn't a lifetime option); whether to have an abortion; what man (if any) to marry; what profession to choose; whether to stay at home with the kids or put career first; or when it's right to give up your whole life for the person you love. Minor choices can be as simple as: Should I drive or walk? If I eat that cake, will I regret it later? The black dress or the red?

As her journey progresses, the Phases of Crossroads encountered by your character will reflect the degree to which she has grown and strengthened. As she gets to know herself better, and develops more internal resources and skills, she is in a better position to face the consequences of actions she will take or once took. What was once an awful dilemma may now not be so critical. Alternatively, a past decision could still be ruining her present peace of mind. As she matures and gets to know herself better, she can make better choices that suit her needs, desires, and chosen identity. Your character will need to somehow make peace with the past if she is to go on without guilt. A female character who is decisive and balanced may make the right decision for herself, but it may be the wrong decision for others.

Crossroads can lead to the Path to Potential and Transition Phases. By making certain choices, the character can enter completely new worlds or ways of being. Making a decision ultimately confronts your character with responsibility for her choice. How she manages that responsibility will be entirely governed by the nature of her personality, her maturity, her personal agency, and the freedoms available to her. The bigger the decision, the more the fallout, the more at risk. She may end up running away. She may "man up." Your protagonist will need to be able to handle it and face the consequences, or she will need to grow.

Examples of Crossroads in Film and TV include: *Saving Mr. Banks*, *Philomena*, *Suffragette*, and *Wild*.

Eruption

The Phase of Eruption reflects your character's need to explode as a reaction to unbearable emotions. Things get too much for all of us, and every now and then, the lid blows! The Phase of Eruption is a potentially cathartic Phase in your character's journey: everything bursts out into the open. It symbolizes an energetic and needed outburst, an emotional, physical, verbal, or social event that leads to change. Usually a tipping point has been reached for the character before this Phase occurs. Eruption is a twofold Phase. First, the lid is blown off. Then the contents settle. The settling can make even more of a mess, with a big impact on your protagonist's journey. The settling, like molten lava, can sweep everyone up and solidify lives in the most unexpected ways.

Trying to please everyone and meet everyone's needs seemingly all of the time can cause major pressure in your female character's life. Multitasking, juggling, and having it all can have their downsides. Your character may be overloaded, or she's the opposite, extremely single-minded, and could erupt at nuisances to her orderly or controlled way of life. Your character might endure an Eruption as a result of being unable to maintain a façade or project a brave face to the world. Too much self-regulation can be a factor. Different cultures have very different modes of expression. How will your character express her need to explode and even lash out? What forms of anger is she permitted to express? Eruption can be fueled by a growing sense of identity crisis. It can seem that every path is blocked, and all your character can do is metaphorically scream out loud. Alternatively she can fight, walk away, or break down. Breakdowns usually lead to breakthroughs — in our own behavior and the behavior of others around us, forcing needed change. Eruptions can happen when we have been misjudged or led astray against our will, or when we have self-regulated for too long.

Eruption is only as healing as your character or other characters want to make it. Some wounds are opened, only to heal over without first expelling the poison. Sometimes a huge mess is left, but your character might move on and let others pick up the pieces. Or she's in a worse position with those she has exposed her difficult emotions to. It's a bit like throwing your cards on the table. The truth is out for all to see, and there's no going back to the same game. The opposite scenario of a character crying for help would be a character erupting out of a need to escape, literally or metaphorically.

The Phase of Eruption can be very short indeed. The eruption could be instant, almost out of nowhere. Your character might suffer a momentary lack of impulse control, setting a spiral of events in motion and/or letting others see her in another light. She might lash out or shoot someone, and surprise herself (and us) in the process. A fight between two characters can seem like a Violation Phase, but sometimes the Violation is only the tipping point that can lead to the protagonist erupting. A steely, repressed character might erupt in a smoldering way rather than a major blast. The impact can be equally powerful.

Eruptions are highly dramatic, so place them wisely. Too many, they lose their dramatic power. Remember when your protagonist powerfully erupts, it's generally because she simply cannot take any more.

Examples of Eruption in film and TV include *Saving Mr. Banks*, *Frances Ha*, *Maleficent*, and *Orange Is the New Black*.

Path to Potential

The Phase of Path to Potential symbolizes your character consciously taking a direction, normally in the hope of a certain or positive outcome. Path to Potential is like the connective tissue of your character's journey, linking the Phases of Identity and Relating to each other. They are the times when she is taking steps and striving for something with a sense of purposefulness and the belief that she is doing the right thing, and that there's no going back. Path to Potential can be the decision to go on an entire quest. It can be about opening the window to let in some air. It symbolizes positive energy, hope, and a sense of empowered, personal agency on your character's journey. It's similar to when we set intentions and feel like we have a game plan.

The whole point of this Phase is that your protagonist feels in control, unlike Transition, which is largely driven by forces that are powerful and feel outside oneself, and often involve a loss of identity. By taking the Path to Potential, your character feels like she is making this happen, because she knows who she is and what she wants to achieve. She's taking back control.

The Path to Potential can lead to labyrinths, dead ends, and crossroads. Your character will take many Paths on her journey. She might come up against any number of obstacles during the course of her story, and it's a guaranteed certainty she will if she's really out of touch with her true needs. In this respect, a Path to Potential will only be as helpful to your character as her levels of self-knowledge, skills, understanding, and insight will allow. If she has unresolved issues, the Path to Potential could lead to disaster. Her issues could metaphorically bite her in the ankle, resulting in her limping rather than striding on her path!

Final Paths: Many female-led stories end with the protagonist taking a final Path to Potential. They aren't returning anywhere familiar; they are moving on. They may have found a new sense of identity, but have yet to find a place to which they can belong. Sometimes a character has unfinished business with herself. She's got to keep moving as a process of self-discovery and healing.

Many female protagonists never go home at the end of their story — there is no sense of return as a better and stronger person. Instead, she may be at heart nomadic. Perhaps she is still unsure what she can expect from life or who she is. She might have resolution on some levels, but not all, and she has to keep moving. The Path to Potential leads her to a final Transition phase.

Phases and Theme

Thinking through each Phase and its effect on your female character's emotional identity can help you better develop your theme. This is because Phases ask you to question your stance on certain issues, and this in turn helps you shape what you are really trying to say in your writing, particularly about gender. Phases ask you, the writer, to deal with your female character's identity as a girl or a woman so you know how these might impact her state of mind. As explained, these can include sexuality, gender issues, motherhood, marriage and divorce, work, loss, aging, relationships, and the female body. You'll be having insights about the areas that feel real for your character, and these might inspire your story's theme.

A Phase energizes the story and takes on a unique form because of several unique factors that only the writer controls. These factors are: your heroine's personality, her emotional wounds, her culture, and her opportunities and challenges. As you get to know each Phase, use them to inspire your interpretation of how your heroine might relate to them, and where in the story they might work. You will also be able to increasingly recognize them in the films and shows that you watch.

Phases in a Complex-Linear Film

Looking at the Phases in a nonlinear film will help you simultaneously develop your theme and your heroine's emerging identity in the story. Complex-linear stories, wherein different female characters follow different stories across time, can be particularly good at revealing themes about gendered identity. They expose the massive changes and differences in women's lives across times and places.

PHASES CASE STUDY:
Wild

Wild is a beautiful and sensitive exploration of a very raw and deeply personal journey to healing. The journey is both emotional and physical as Cheryl Strayed walks the Pacific Coast Trail to rediscover herself after the death of her mother, trying to become the woman her mother intended her to be. It is also a way of reliving and being close to her mother, of deeply connecting with the "feminine" by closing off from the real world and allowing nature — the wild — to facilitate her healing process.

Cheryl's journey is both an emotional pilgrimage and a way of honoring her mother. The film unfolds in several timescales, with the linear journey of Cheryl's hike broken up by memories, voices, and images of her childhood, her life as an adult with her mother, her mother's illness and death, and the emotional chaos Cheryl descends into afterward. Cheryl's need to come to terms with the loss of her mother Bobbi is familiar to many stages of Murdock's Heroine's Journey as a process of healing and reconnection with the self. Her "mother/daughter split" (one of Murdock's terms) is on one hand never completed since Cheryl lived closely with Bobbi, a single mother who fled her violent husband. Bobbi even enrolled as a mature student at the same college as Cheryl. Their enforced separation happens when Bobbi is diagnosed with cancer and survives only three months. Bobbi's death sends Cheryl into a dark descent of drugs and casual sex. When she hits rock bottom, she has an urgent need to "reconnect with the feminine," and decides to undertake the grueling hike. Throughout the hike, she heals the literal "mother-daughter split," and finally emerges a more integrated human being who has forgiven herself.

As a highly emotional journey in which searching for a sense of identity is crucial for the protagonist, *Wild* provides a rich and fertile case study for the Phases model.

Transition

In terms of identity, Cheryl is lost when she starts the hike. She is rootless, needing to rely on her divorced husband's mailing address. She is no longer a literature student. She is no longer a wife. She is not in contact with her brother, who was equally traumatized by their mother's death. Cheryl literally has no place she wants to belong to in the outside world. The transition is the hike and her time in the wild. It will take her from one state of being to another if she manages to honor her mother and heal herself. She knows she cannot move on until she's made sense of the past. In that sense, she is in emotional freefall, out of the nightmare of compulsive self-destruction, but with no clear understanding of whom she might become now that she has lost her previous self. She is in Transition as a person, a woman, a lover, and a daughter. She is lost to herself. The hike itself provides many minor Transitions as the physical landscape and the humans and creatures she encounters change — and Cheryl has to take risks and adapt.

Maternal Lessons

Powerful features of Cheryl's memories are the words and messages spoken by her mother Bobbi. These are shown in fragmentary or longer flashbacks cutting or flowing into Cheryl's present. Cheryl remembers Bobbi's worldview, her way of coping with what Cheryl's former self saw as a bad and extremely difficult life. She would angrily challenge Bobbi's positive attitude. *How can I see the bright side of things when my life is terrible?* she would demand of her mother. Bobbi responds with an absence of regret, empowered because she birthed Cheryl and her brother, the best things to ever happen to her. She tells her daughter to see the good, choose the sunshine, make time for beauty, and fulfill her potential. The journey allows Cheryl to re-listen to these spoken Maternal Lessons from the perspective of one who is now ready to hear. The indirect Maternal Lesson that Cheryl comes to terms with is that if you don't value and respect yourself, you may trash yourself or let yourself be trashed by others. In some ways, Cheryl's bout of heroin abuse and sex mirrors her mother's Violation Phase of low self-esteem as an abused wife. Neither Cheryl nor Bobbi ever consciously identify as victims, although society would label them as such. This refusal to become a victim is an important Maternal Lesson for Cheryl.

Father Distance

Cheryl's actual father, glimpsed through impressionistic images only, was clearly a scary and violent man who Bobbi fled after being beaten and having her children threatened. The negative father figure creates a mother/daughter relationship that might actually be too close and co-dependent (Murdock's "identification with the feminine") until cancer forces them apart. Cheryl hasn't been able to learn to find her own identity beyond the protective family unit. Her engagement as a student is fragile, and she gives up. Cheryl consequently relates sexually to men in unhealthy ways, reflecting her distrust of men and the self-hatred she feels. She compulsively cheats on her husband until he wants out of the marriage. On the trail, she encounters both caring and hostile men as embodiments of positive and negative masculinity, thus experiencing longer and shorter phases of Father Distance. Men as nurturers come in the form of other hikers willing to help her with practical matters. Greg, a random hiker, sees she has beaten herself up a lot and shows compassion. A farmer helps her early on, taking her home for food and a hot shower.

Cheryl's "masculine" heroic quest, to actually do the hike, bonds her with the other male hikers, who accept her into their fraternity. She holds her own with them. In therapy, expressing hostility toward her male therapist, Cheryl angrily remembers a period of her life marked by her father's abuse and abandonment. Father Distance comes in the form of actual and potential violation by men. First, in Cheryl's memory of her father's fist in her face, and also in the form of two men who hassle and threaten her on the trail.

Adornment
Cheryl's body image reflects her mixed emotions. Her attitude to her body expresses her inner turmoil, her guilt, and her pain. She and her soon-to-be ex-husband have "divorce" tattoos honoring the love they had. Later, Cheryl's body is covered with sores left by her rucksack and her boots. On the final stretch of the hike, she heads into a motel and dresses up for a night out at a bar where a band is playing. Looking and feeling refreshed, she is attracted to a nice man and has "healthy" sex; she is in control of her desires, and he sees her as a person (unlike the sex-with-strangers period she went through in her darkest days). They make love in a sensitive way.

Self-Regulation
Cheryl's memories include a moment where Cheryl, with her student friends, passes Bobbi in college. Cheryl is embarrassed,

and practically ignores her mother. Later she apologizes. Overall, Cheryl's journey tends to include self-regulation only at moments she feels out of her depth or wary, such as when she's with strange men who she fears. She also self-regulates slightly in company with hikers, reflecting caution of herself and others around men. However, as she is primarily on a mission to find herself, to heal and become whole, she largely avoids self-regulating. She is on a journey to self-acceptance, so it is important to her to be real and in the moment.

Desire for Union

The hike presents an intense yearning for reliving her life with Bobbi and making sense of the loss. By journeying into the wilderness, alone, Cheryl can be with her mother again in her memories. She remembers Bobbi's smile, her dancing, holding her as a baby, and other special memories.

Loving Too Much

After the loss of her mother, Cheryl goes through a phase of Loving Too Much, with her robotic sex addiction linked to her use of heroin. It is completely self-destructive, opening her up to all manner of risks like disease, overdose, and violence. She has sex with any man who is up for it. The sex is raw, urgent, seedy, and often in squalid situations like alleys or crack dens.

Violation

The extreme endurance hiking the trail demands is violating: Cheryl's body suffers from hunger, sores, and lost toenails. There is an element of penance in Cheryl's subjection to the wild and its tough, painful, and treacherous demands. Whereas she allowed herself to be violated by others through sex and injecting heroin to numb herself from pain, hiking the trail is the opposite type of antidote; the violation of the wild helps her finally confront her memories of emotional trauma. It is like the pain of rebreaking a bone so that it may heal properly. She is the walking wounded, walking her way to healing.

Crossroads

The trail presents many crossroads, physically. Literally, Cheryl faces dilemmas of her own making (taking the wrong gas for her camping stove), and frequently evaluates whether she should turn back. She faces blockages on the paths, different routes she has to take, different obstacles (like snakes), and far scarier ones like potential rapists. These numerous physical crossroads present her with a series of choices that form part of the healing process. She has to make decisions about the best ways to stay safe and healthy, and about who is to be trusted and who is to be avoided.

Eruption

Cheryl's biggest eruption happens when she utters a primal scream across the desert after losing a walking boot, having ripped off her toenail. This is the first dramatic scene of the film. At the time, we put her rage and agony down to sheer frustration. It carries with it an instantaneous moment of self-Violation as she removes her nail. Later, when the story revisits this moment, we understand the deeper reasons behind the scream. She is really screaming in rage that her mother's life was cut short. It is the anger of loss and mourning, and the past can never be undone.

Path to Potential

Deciding to hike the trail reflects Cheryl's decision to sort herself out. Because she has lost her identity, she knows she is incapable of anything beyond a healing process, one that enables her to accept her pain. The wild offers her a chance to retreat from life, to confront her demons, to face her memories. In this respect, Cheryl is in control and has a plan. Path to

Potential is the final leg of the journey: Cheryl is now able to enter civilization and begin to live again as the sophisticated, intelligent woman her mother raised her to be.

How *you* as a writer experience each Phase is shaped by the SuperThemes influencing you, your character's personality, the Role-Choices she is embracing at any given moment, and the themes you are exploring through your character's journey. She might be identifying with a certain Role-Choice, but a Phase will show the details of how she relates to it and what she does with it. For example, if she identifies as a weak and helpless Victim who doesn't know how to ask for support, she may be more prone to Retreat too quickly from life, with distrust of others. She may self-sabotage and be lonely. Alternatively, a rigid, righteous Caryatid may have no problem with self-regulating. In fact, she could be so good at it, she doesn't know how to let go. She may need a good Eruption!

CHAPTER 5

Women in Trouble:
Conflict and Female Protagonists

Conflict is basically a clash between two opposing view-points. That clash can be physical, mental, verbal, emotional, relational, territorial, ideological, political, national and international, and even intergalactic. Conflict can be healthy, destructive, annihilating, preventable, unnecessary, or necessary. Conflict is part of life. How you manage conflict in your own life will depend on your personality, your belief system, and your self-control. It will depend equally on the support systems and access to power you have. Even if you choose a peaceful path in life, conflict can follow you. Your relationship might suddenly end; you might lose a loved one, your job, your money, or your health; you might be attacked, physically, sexually, or verbally. Your country might go to war. All these can and do present obstacles in our lives; they are part of being human. An attitude of acceptance, tolerance, and forgiveness might help you get through the conflict, but the conflict still has to be borne in some way. And of course, this is all exactly the same for your character!

When it comes to stories, we're often told that conflict is the primary building block of all drama, whatever the subgenre. A dearth of conflict makes a story boring. *What's at stake? What's the threat? What does she have to lose? Who's the bad guy?* These are familiar and often very important questions in the writing process. If you're writing a female-driven story, conflict can come in gender-skewed forms, reflecting differences in the lives of and expectations on your female characters, but also as a result of how you depict the obstacles and difficulties for females. It's up to you as the writer to work out how the conflict in your story plays out.

Conflict and Gender

As mentioned earlier, you may be choosing a female protagonist because it is actually easier for you to explore strongly emotional stories through a female character. You may simply believe female audiences want emotionally compelling stories because females are "better" at articulating their emotional angst, or are at least more interested in stories that focus on struggles with finding happiness. You may be choosing conflicts of a more emotional nature. Alternatively, you may be putting your female protagonist on a quest of supreme danger, with monumental, life-threatening external conflicts.

How your character reacts as a woman to the various conflicts you develop will reveal some of your own gender biases. For example, if you belong to a culture where boys/ men aren't supposed to cry and don't easily share or articulate their fears and vulnerabilities, you may reveal this in your writing by giving more emotional angst to your female characters. They might express fear and emotion more openly. They might be more helpless. They might be saved by tough guys. Or you may want to subvert the gender patterns, and your female character is the one that holds things together and does the saving, including male characters who are helpless.

Conflict and Genre

Whatever genre you choose for your female-driven story, conflict needs to work within the conventions of that genre. If you are pushing the boundaries of conflict in terms of genre, then you need to pull it off in a brilliant, rather than jarring, way. For instance, a romantic comedy that includes the female protagonist self-mutilating potentially takes it into a darker and more dramatic terrain. You will need to work hard to make tonal inconsistency work. Broadly speaking, for the different tones that conflict to work well together, you need to ensure that there is an overall consistency throughout your story. The Layers of Conflict model may help you identify the broad parameters of the conflict in your female character's journey, and that will suit your genre. It may help you decide which conflicts are most important to you and your message, and what your story is really exploring through this character's experiences.

Cultural Conflict

The first thing to be aware of is how your own cultural attitudes and expectations are going to have an impact on your writing. Your own cultural values will affect:

* Your female character's culture, the one she has always known, might not be the one that she feels she truly belongs to

* The culture of the audience you want to reach

Using conflict effectively boils down to working out how you want your audience to react to your female character's situation. Ask yourself:

- Do you want your audience to sympathize with your character's plight?

- Do you want your audience to question her motives, and hope that she sees the light?

- Do you want her to transform the world she lives in so she can be free in any area of her life?

- Do you want your audience to question the values of the world we live in?

- Do you want to push the buttons of your audience by shocking them?

Personal Agency

Conflict, and its opposite dramatic element Union (discussed in the next chapter), can be hugely affected by your protagonist's sense of "personal agency" in terms of when, where, and how she feels able to have power. At the broadest level, this is your character's sense of autonomy. Thinking through ways in which your character has personal agency can help you develop nuance and dimension, particularly when thinking through antagonistic factors in your character's life. This, in turn, can help you minimize unsubtle and predictable negative forces. Identifying these can be a useful aspect of the character-development process.

Use the following checklist to brainstorm your protagonist's personal agency.

Territory

Humans are territorial beings. We like to have a place to call our own where we create the rules and control what goes on. It can be a physical location, a room, a book, or an imaginary place.

It could be the open road. Ask: Where does your protagonist belong? Where does she feel comfortable to be herself, or truly safe? Where does she retreat? What place is hers and hers alone? Does she even have freedom of movement? If your character doesn't have any territory, why not? Is there a territorial gender division in her world? Territory at its broadest also includes her material economy. What does she own? What can she trade?

Dignity

Self-esteem is dependent on factors that encourage a sense of personal dignity. Dignity is based on being respected, having autonomy, having equal rights, feeling assured that one has a voice in the matters that are fundamental to one's security. It is about being valued as an individual with rights. Ask yourself: What gives your character a sense of personal dignity? What does dignity mean to her? Who respects her, and how is this respect conveyed? How is her sense of dignity threatened? Are women respected in her society, or do misogynistic forces erode their senses of self-worth? How do these play out?

Creativity

Being free to create and imagine is central to being human. It is an impulse and a drive that we all share and need. It is vital to happiness, enabling a sense of hope and freedom. Creative impulses demand freedom and the ability to immerse oneself without distractions or the overly familiar, mundane demands of life. Ask yourself where your protagonist is safe to feel free, explore, have fun, and play. What triggers her creative impulses, and what form do they take? What inhibits her creative self? As a female, is she an enabler of others' creativity and pursuits, or is she able to take space for herself?

Vitality

Vitality is not about just being healthy. It's about life-force and strength, and can be a mental as much as a physical state of being. Having vitality is essential to ambition and drive, as it is the energy source that makes hopes and dreams possible. What makes your character feel strong and alive? What gives her energy and vigor? What factors work against her vital self? As a female, does she exercise, compete in sports, get enough nourishment? Does she deny herself? Does she have opportunities to develop vitality? Is she physically challenged, and how does she cope with this to feel empowered and able? What drains or saps her?

The Layers of Conflict

The Layers of Conflict is a model that can help you work out the obstacles that could be operating on and impacting your character's life. By getting to know the layers of conflict, and learning how they can function in your story, you can make sure conflict is working to support all of your intentions for your character and her journey. For example, if you want to write about a girl's emotional and physical battle with bulimia, then it's a good idea to think about how her problem is affected by her closest relationships, her family, her community, and the wider culture. Most fundamentally, you will be asking yourself what internal problems she has that cause her to be bulimic. Where in her life is she conflicted, and why?

By thinking each layer through, you will be able to make the right creative choices for your story. The layers of conflict can help you strengthen your characters so you really know what each one is up against. They can also help you intensify your story's theme and metaphoric wound.

The layers of conflict are:

- Layer One: Internal Conflict
- Layer Two: Significant Other Conflict

- Layer Three: Friends and Family Conflict

- Layer Four: Community Conflict

- Layer Five: Culture Conflict

- Layer Six: Nation Conflict

- Layer Seven: World Conflict

The aim of the Layer model is to help you weave as many forms of conflict into each scene as you can to enrich and deepen your story. The level of complexity you develop will ultimately be defined by the genre and the tone of your story, as well as the nature of your main target audience. Too many internal conflicts would be lost on a children's audience, for example. Conversely, we expect substantially complex conflicts affecting the main characters in long-running TV drama series.

The Layers of Conflict Diagram

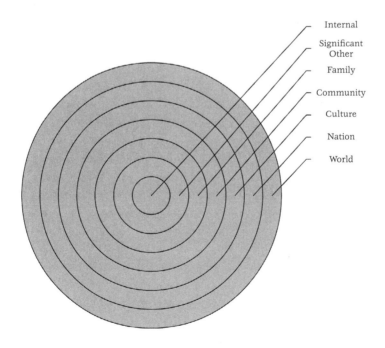

LAYER ONE —
Internal Conflict

This layer reflects the most private, deepest *internal conflict* your character feels. It represents her most private self. It is the scar tissue that she tries to hide from the world. Female protagonists who are emotionally wounded, trapped in a situation or a culture that damages their sense of identity, who have a battle between expectations and how they really want to live their lives, or who have deep ambivalence about the choices they are faced with are all experiencing internal conflict. The thing about internal conflicts is that they are really hard for your character to be aware of. Very few of us fully articulate our internal angst, and if we do, it is with people we trust.

An internal conflict is ultimately a vulnerability; to open up requires feelings of safety. Internal conflict is the hardest conflict to write because it is the thoughts and feelings going on inside your character's mind, even those she cannot admit to herself. Most emotional journeys are concerned with healing these conflicts and bringing them out into the open. Being healed (or not) depends on the circumstances and the theme of your story; your character rarely starts out with deep emotional truth or an ability to choose a better way of life. This internal world is where you will do most of your most challenging hard work to develop your screenplay! Your task as writer is to develop this internal world, aware that there is never just "one" internal conflict, and then to define ways it may be manifesting in and affecting the character's external world.

Stories that emphasize internal conflict above all other layers can be very powerful viewing experiences because so much is going on beneath the surface. The subtext is richer because so much is left unsaid; conflicts between people are all the more complex because they do not reveal who they are, often because they may not even know themselves on a deep level. As a writer, the more internal conflict you develop, the better you will be at showing, not telling. Internal conflict is the hardest to write.

Let's consider some internal conflicts.

Internal Conflict	Manifested As
Lack of self-awareness	Being out of kilter, putting oneself in jeopardy, attracting unhealthy relationships
Shame	Fearing exposure, addiction, avoiding intimacy, self-harming
Regret/Failure	Depression, no ambition, envy of others, avoiding opportunities
Low self-esteem	Destructive relationships, unhealthy lifestyle, unhelpful decisions, eating disorders, self-harm

How your character emotionally copes with her internal conflicts will very much depend on her particular psychology. Knowing some basic principles about the psychodynamics of conflict can really help you build her internal world. They are the ways the character has developed to deal with life. Understanding them will help you work out how each of the more "outer" layers of conflict affect her. It's important to remember that your character might experience each of these psychodynamics at different stages in the story. Different situations might provoke different reactions. But it will take a lot of growth on the journey for your character to actually change some deeply rooted ways of relating.

The psychodynamic processes that are really helpful in developing characters' interactions are:

- Projection
- Denial
- Repression

Let's take a look at each one in more detail.

Projection — all about self-protection

Very often we blame or accuse others of having bad qualities or traits that we actually have ourselves. This is projection. Projection basically protects us from self-criticism. It helps us survive the horror of being ourselves and our living with our dark sides. Characters who project a lot can be very frustrating for others to be around because they have a lack of self-truth, and they find it difficult to see their part in a situation. They can be very manipulative. Or they are simply very scared. Normally they project a lot because they don't have high self-esteem or much self-awareness. Not all accusations are projection, however. Sometimes a character might be making a really good point about another character's limitations, or an unfair situation. This is why projection is a complex dynamic for a female character if her world isn't equal. She may find fault with what's holding her back, but could get stuck in blaming everything else because she is angry with her own failure to take action.

This sense of unfairness can play itself out in intimate relationships in emotional journeys. A female character might feel like the victim in a relationship because she is burdened with children or housework, or because men earn more or are promoted before her.

Your character might unconsciously be carrying around some emotional wounds from the past. Her way of dealing with these might be to project all those aspects of herself onto other people. However, it's important to remember that if she is projecting, then she's learned to do this for a reason.

This is how the psychodynamic of projection can play out: A character projects:

self-hate	as	a belief that somebody else hates her
anger	as	an accusation that others are angry
self-pity	as	a conviction that others are victimizing her
selfishness	as	a belief everyone else is selfish

Denial

Because women tend to find it easier to share emotions, they might get more opportunity for realizing they are denying, but a female "denier" can equal her male counterpart any day. Deniers deny as a defense mechanism to maintain control and power and to hide deep feelings of anxiety. It is a need to be thought of as strong so as to not be hurt. It's not so much about putting on a mask; it's about really believing that the best face to show herself and others is a strong one. Characters who deny bad stuff are generally quite good at getting ahead, and can be positive thinkers. This is a good quality. "You are your thoughts" is a basic principle of self-awareness, and characters who deny can prove that positive thinking is the way to go. However, there is a destructive side to denial. Characters who deny a lot aren't always empathetic, as seeing other perspectives can be hard for them. They don't want to get their hands dirty with other people's pain or misery. They don't mind power, but responsibility isn't really their thing.

A character who *denies* will say:

I'm not angry	to really mean	you want to bug me but you can't
I'm not jealous	to really mean	I'm not going to show you I'm hurt
It's not so bad	to really mean	don't pry into my affairs

Repression

Women who repress their true emotions have generally been taught that their feelings are not important or worthy of consideration. They can have terribly low esteem, or have been damaged by abusive situations they haven't been able to heal. For these kinds of female characters, repression is a safer bet than facing or reliving their emotional trauma. A repressive character usually develops elaborate ways of hiding her emotional scars, and thinks she's convinced everyone that they aren't there — even when the signs are obvious to the people close to her. Trauma is usually accompanied by shock. If a fairly well-adjusted character suffers a violating trauma in adult life (such as torture, violence, or rape), she might repress it, even if this goes against her natural openness. If she has no one to trust, or comes from a culture that doesn't permit communication with strangers, then she might not get the support she needs.

A character who represses is scarred by:

Fear of abandonment	could show it by	being dependent, no autonomy
Humiliation	could show it by	self-mutilation, eating disorders
Sexual abuse	could show it by	false sexuality, pleasing others

Loss	could show it by	anger, guilt, exhaustion
Trauma	could show it by	withdrawal, numbness, insecurity
Guilt	could show it by	too much responsibility, enabling

Think about Internal Conflicts as being the private wounds that the character doesn't easily face or share. The more complex your character's internal conflicts are, the more dimensional she will be. They will help you create interesting and unique ways for your character to deal with the next layers of conflict in her life, which are all external.

Layer Two —
Significant Other Conflict

The Second Layer relates to the conflict generated by your character's relationship with her *significant other*. This does not have to be her lover. It can be the person who takes up most of her headspace and gives her the most headaches. It can be the person she is trying to be close to, the person with whom she has the most longstanding relationship (good or bad), or the person she is leaving. It can also be a parent, a child, a sibling, a boss, a colleague — it entirely depends on your story. Or there may be several significant others, like a sorority such as a group of friends. In TV series, the significant other may in fact shift each episode.

The conflict generated by this important and primary relationship can take many forms. These include wanting to love or be loved; not realizing they are in love; parent/child dynamics; professional rivalry; betrayal; jealousy; envy; loss; abuse; and victimization. It can be a rite of passage, such as marriage, birth, divorce, loss, or death. It covers the whole range of emotions that the significant other can trigger in your character.

It is rare for female-driven stories not to have conflict presented by a significant other. Love and romance are central to human existence, but often the love storyline can be less important and present fewer problems to a male hero than the external quest he faces.

LAYER THREE —
Family and Friends Conflict

The Third Layer relates to your protagonist's family and friends — the groups she is most attached to for support or out of obligation — and the problems that this group can generate, either as individuals or as the collective. The "family" can mean those people your character considers to be her real family. As many female-driven stories involve family, they can be a common source of conflict. As female characters are given more external quests, the prominence of the family might diminish.

Family conflict can simply take the form of unresolved issues in your character's backstory, and these can spill out into the story as her way of handling problems in the here and now. The family is often the cause of the internal conflicts she experiences. Family life gives your character her earliest experiences and role models. Orphans, adopted children, and sci-fi "manufactured" children will have wildly different experiences with family life.

How your story represents the family values you believe in will often by evident by the conflicts your character experiences with the family. If she has been abused by the family, you might be making a thematic point around the causes of that abuse. Are the individuals just plain bad, or is the family disadvantaged in some way, and dysfunction is thus a product of social and economic factors? Is there a cycle of deprivation in the family that your character is attempting to break? Does her family represent the family womb or the family tomb?

If the family is partly or mainly in the backstory, then your female character is likely to have some form of friends, allies, and supporters. If not, and she is an Outsider Heroine, then what are the factors behind her lack of a supportive group? Friends, despite their good intentions, can cause all kinds of problems: not being there enough, being too interfering, knowing the character too well, or *thinking* that they know the character too well. They can embark on misguided interventions for the protagonist, ones that completely backfire. Or else they can be completely two-faced, or downright betrayers. The revelation of a false friend can be a painful process to endure; likewise the realization that somebody is a flaky friend or only wants the relationship on their terms to meet their needs.

LAYER FOUR —
Community Conflict

The Fourth Layer relates to the community your character belongs to. This can be the actual local area, like her town or village, her apartment block, or her work environment. It's basically her life in a wider setting, beyond the emotional sphere of significant others, friendship groups, and the family environment. If her significant other is someone she works with, then lots of additional conflict can be caused in her professional community. Problems can take the form of professional rivalry; failure; loss of status in the community; not fitting in with the community's values and mores; and annihilation of the community through war or illness. Many tragic love stories are caused by the family and the community not being able to tolerate the female protagonist's love affair.

LAYER FIVE —
Culture Conflict

Cultural values can cause big problems for your protagonist if she goes against the grain, or is motivated to champion change through revolution, however personal. The problems caused by cultural values can create a lot of internal conflict if the character feels unable to meet others' expectations, comply, or fit in.

The pressure to marry, to stay married, and be a good mother can create massive problems for your character. Sexism, racism, and other forms of discrimination are also cultural conflicts that may limit her opportunities or be damaging in other ways. She may fight them or internalize them, and feel ashamed, linking her internal conflicts to the wider world. Being from a respectable family, having the right education, knowing social etiquette, and having money and status symbols are either a result of privilege, hard work, or luck. It is very easy to fall on the wrong side of the tracks, and getting across may prove very difficult for your character. It is even harder if she was born on the wrong side, and her society doesn't allow much social or economic mobility.

LAYER SIX —
Nation Conflict

The wider political events that are happening in the time and place your character lives may provide a range of conflicts for her, directly and indirectly. A country's legal and political system will shape your female character's life in numerous ways, depending on her age, ethnicity, ability, and socioeconomic status. Consider reproductive rights versus equality in the workplace. Your character may be a politician, a crusader, or a campaigner, bringing her into direct confrontation with others. She may be part of a diaspora that needs to migrate to or seek sanctuary in another country for safety. Perhaps the host country is hostile or alienating. Perhaps it is welcoming, and she cannot adjust or is suspicious.

Does she live in an equal society? Is her country at work? Does she live in a utopian world that you have invented? It's a good idea to identify the dominant form of rule, such as democracy, oligarchy, plutocracy, anarchy, or totalitarian state. Is it a capitalist or socialist system? Who holds power, and how are the forces of power accountable?

Depending on the genre, you will be building a world that influences all inhabitants, positively and negatively.

LAYER SEVEN —
World Conflict

Turbulence in the world can impact your story and character directly or indirectly. Stories can take on wider dimensions if a sense of the global order can somehow be conveyed. All countries have a specific position in the world order. War and science-fiction films are the most emblematic of the kinds of conflicts that are generated by turbulence in the world. Consider how international conflicts impact your character directly and indirectly. If she is in the army or some kind of warrior, what is she fighting for? Fictional worlds can be exciting and liberating to create, particularly if gender neutrality is important to you. There are no restrictions on how worlds operate, or how nations or other entities cooperate (or not).

~ EXERCISE ~
Finding the Layers of Conflict

First, brainstorm all the layers of conflict in your story. This might hopefully trigger some great insights. It doesn't matter if you aren't quite sure yet, but try to identify how all the layers might be symbolized in the story. The process will help you decide which layers of conflict are most important to focus on.

Then, imagining yourself in the shoes of your female protagonist, complete the WHAT'S THE PROBLEM? QUESTIONNAIRE.

What's The Problem?
~ QUESTIONNAIRE ~

1. Who or what is your biggest problem? Why?
2. What gets in the way of you living your life exactly how you want to?
3. Who or what do you dislike in your family?
4. How do you feel about how other family members treat you?
5. What is your deepest cause of unhappiness?
6. What can you do about this?
7. Who takes up most of your thoughts? Why do they?
8. What are the main causes of problems in your closest relationships?
9. What are your problems at work? How can you change these?
10. If you could turn back the clock in any area of your life to do things differently, what would they be? How would you change things?

CASE STUDY:

Layers of Conflict in *Maleficent*

Maleficent is an imaginative and fantastical retelling of the Sleeping Beauty fairy tale from the point of view of the evil fairy Maleficent. Maleficent curses the infant Princess Aurora at her christening with the threat that on her sixteenth birthday Aurora will prick her finger and fall into a slumber that can only be ended by "true love's kiss." The story reveals why Maleficent becomes so bitter in the first place, leading to this harsh curse, and how she resolves her pain and anger to find love and contentment.

Internal Conflicts

Maleficent has no extreme internal conflicts at the beginning of her story. She is happy and content in her kingdom, The Moors, where all the creatures live in harmony, respectful of one another. It is a benign matriarchy where Maleficent is seen as a leader, no doubt due to her powers. Maleficent is loved but there is a hint of some inner loneliness, which makes her vulnerable to the charms of a human boy who comes to Maleficent's attention when he steals from The Moors.

Maleficent's internal conflicts develop as her relationship with Princess Aurora grows. She is **conflicted: she wants to hate her, but the baby is adorable** and likes Maleficent. When the fairy godmothers set up home in the woods to care for the baby Aurora (at the behest of King Stephan, to avoid the finger-pricking curse coming true), Maleficent experiences something of a **moral dilemma**. As the fairies are hopeless at childcare, Maleficent has to step in secretly on several occasions, torn between a desire to see the child dead and her higher self's wish to protect this joyous bundle of love. As Aurora grows up, and develops a relationship with Maleficent, she believes Maleficent is her fairy godmother, sent to protect her. Maleficent holds back, again **feeling torn**. She doesn't want to love Aurora, but the relationship with Aurora makes her very happy. This generates complex feelings in Maleficent, such as **guilt** that gets so bad that she tries to revoke her own curse, but fails. She feels **remorseful** when the curse is fulfilled and Aurora falls asleep. Maleficent is **angry with herself**.

Significant Other Conflicts

Stephan, as a boy, lets Maleficent down. She loves him, but he becomes **too obsessed by ambition**, and his visits to The Moors become less frequent. Her feelings toward him make her **vulnerable** to his treachery. He cannot resist the King's pledge that whomever kills Maleficent will be made king, but he cannot bring himself to kill Maleficent. Instead, he **brutalizes her** by cutting off her wings. This is a **dreadful trauma** for Maleficent; she is left to wander with a stick, her **loss and devastation** slowly turning to **bitterness and anger**. The assault is not only physical, it is mentally cruel — how could someone she loved do that to her?

Discovering Stephan has had a baby, she is again wounded. She vows to **hit him where it hurts**, his daughter being sent to sleep forever; as far as Maleficent is concerned, true love cannot exist, so a true love's kiss cannot either. She is **poisoned and hurt** to the core. Her emotions of betrayal **fester inside her**, changing her. She wants to hate the baby princess, nicknaming her Beastie, but finds **it impossible**. As her love for Aurora grows, Stephan's **hate and fear** of Maleficent increases. He is made **obsessional by hate**, now determined to **kill** her. His hatred is pathological, suggesting he is **projecting his guilt** (an internal conflict) by manifesting it with a need to destroy, to alleviate this hell of his own making. When Aurora falls asleep, it is only Maleficent's kiss, the loving kiss of a fairy godmother, which rouses her. Maleficent is in the Castle when she does so, and Stephan traps her, **determined to kill her**.

He is **deranged and beyond reason**, and Maleficent must fight the man she once loved **to the death**.

Friends and Family Conflict

Theo is Maleficent's ally, a fairy crow. He challenges Maleficent's motives, trying to appeal to her higher self when she is at her darkest and most angry. He **knows her very well**, which is irritating to Maleficent as he can **confront** her easily.

Community Conflict

The Moors are **plunged into darkness** by Maleficent, and where the creatures once loved Maleficent, and everyone lived in sunny harmony, now they are **hurt and fearful** of her darkness.

Culture Conflict

The values of The Moors are based on equality, the right to life, and freedom. When the boy Stephan steals a jewel, Maleficent instructs him to put it back. This transaction symbolizes the conflict between The Moors and the human Kingdom. Later, Maleficent's reign of anger creates values that are at odds with her "good" magical powers and the values of the matriarchal world to which she belongs. She becomes a **dark fairy**, using her powers to self-protect, to curse, **to inflict damage**, to close down, **to create barriers and walls**. She mirrors the **fearful values** of the human culture. Wings symbolize the freedom of The Moors' values, and without her wings, Maleficent **cannot feel safe** in the world. She **abandons** her values.

National Conflict

Stephan becomes a cruel king, driving his ironworkers too hard, generating **fear and distrust** in his kingdom. Likewise, Maleficent **plunges The Moors into darkness**.

International Conflict

The aggressive male kings **wage war** against Maleficent, **threatened** by a matriarchal world they do not understand, and **greedy** for the riches contained within the lands of The Moors.

CHAPTER 6

〰〰〰

Feeling Good and Finding Love:
Working with Union

Harmony, connection, intimacy, reciprocity, and love are all essential to the emotional journeys that many female protagonists take. Read most screenwriting books, and the mantra is *Conflict, Conflict, Conflict* — or the focus is on obstacles, tests, and challenges. From Aristotle onward, no conflict equals no story. The bottom line is that the focus on conflict negates other equally important human needs. The ability to let a baby grow in your own body and feel good about it is the deepest source of Union. Nurturing a child, whether it is breastfeeding, diaper changing, reading a bedtime story, or constantly trying to shape your offspring's perspective, is being in a state of Union with another. Perhaps "masculine" theories about storytelling have overlooked Union because, up until fairly recently, men have traditionally excluded themselves from the hands-on side of caregiving and nurturing others. Masculine-oriented cultures penned by writers often make female characters carry the caring and nurturing roles. Conflict is, of course, vital to storytelling. But it's time to elevate the principle of Union to its rightful place in the dramatic tradition. As often as we say, "What's at stake? What are the obstacles?" we should also be asking, "Where is she safe? What's helping her?" Let's start saying *No Union, no story!*

Union is, at the most basic level, the flipside of conflict. Union can mean joy, it can mean peace, and it can mean harmony. It can also mean the coming together of two characters, or a group of people, who feel truly connected with each other. Union essentially means being as one. It is the deepest human need, yet one that takes a myriad of forms in our stories. So why is it that as a dramatic principle Union is so overwhelmingly overlooked? Linda Seger made this point in *When Women Call the Shots*. She asked lots of women filmmakers (writers, directors, and producers) how they felt their stories were different than men's. Harmony was a big issue for many of these women. The principle of Union is extremely important to many female-driven stories and genres that appeal to female audiences. In fact, it can sometimes seem like an overriding principle. It's true that many women like stories that explore love, even if it's love gone wrong. Female audiences can be fond of deeply emotional stories where the heroine experiences relationships, including highs and lows such as happiness, loss, caring, warmth, intimacy, and commitment — the joyful aspects of being in a family or relationship.

Conventional "masculine" identity deals out different kinds of conflict for characters. These entail goals; quests; learning to be there for others through a lonely road of trials; hierarchical power structures; and the need to protect, save, and provide materially for others. Achieving status is a lonely battle fraught with competition and rivalry. Men may still feel def... their work, whereas women's external identity may...

considered important by themselves or others. As men take on more roles that were once seen as traditionally feminine, it's no coincidence that their stories are showing more aspects of Union. Expressions of joy are seen less as women's emotional stuff, and more "human." Writers have cottoned onto the fact they are depriving their male characters of the sheer bliss of caring, sharing, and loving — each other. At last they are giving themselves permission to express joy, happiness, and the beauty of friendship.

As a writer, you might believe that women are the ones who promote bonds and provide the nurturing. Or you might feel that women hadn't really had much choice but to marry well and become nurturers until they fought for independence and equal rights. Maybe you are evolution-minded as a story-teller and feel women's need to have babies to keep the human tribe going makes them want stories about finding and keeping love. Or you might feel that both men and women have exactly the same needs for Union in the form of love, harmony, peace, and joy.

How you personally feel about the joyous and Union-filled aspects in stories will very much depend on your own attitude about Union. For instance, if you are someone who recoils at overt, joyous femininity, you might feel very uncomfortable around emotional expression. If you basically prefer more "masculine" stories where action, power, control, and conflict are dominant in the storytelling, you might cringe at too much Union as a hallmark of "feminine" storytelling. The over-Layering of Union in genres such as comedies and romcoms might be off-putting to you. This is where the terms "chick lit" and "chick flick" emerged from, labeling anything about relationships as women's light and fluffy stuff.

But many writers love Union, and you could be one of them. It could be one of the reasons you chose a female protagonist anyway, because you like emotionally driven, "caring" stories with lots of Union; and to you, a female character just feels more appropriate for these. Some female audiences, encouraged by cultural expectations to identify with Union, may crave stories that reflect joy, harmony, happiness, and love. The big romantic epics, for example. Others may prefer dark and dangerous crime! As audiences like to pick and choose, we as writers do the same. You might write a string of dark stories, only to want to next explore something lighter and happier. Of course these are generalizations. We live in postmodern times where anything goes. But if you have strong feelings about union, you might want to ask yourself why. Why does it make you cringe? Why do you think it's important? How will union help you build your story's message and themes in the same way that conflict does?

The Layers of Union

Your role as writer is to work out what emotional well-being means for your female character, how she is going to achieve it (if she is), and who and what the biggest external contributory factors to her happiness are. Are joy and harmony expressed differently by your characters? What are the cultural nuances affecting you and your characters? You can do this by a exploring and developing the principle of Union in your story. How your character relates to all the Layers of Union is important for you to know so you can weave them appropriately into your story. Genre and tone will influence the way you depict union in your story in much the same way as conflict does.

Just like you can work out the Layers of Conflict in your story, you may wish to explore and get to know the Layers of Union.

The Layers of Union are:

- Layer One: Internal Union
- Layer Two: Significant Other Union
- Layer Three: Family Union
- Layer Four: Community Union
- Layer Five: Culture Union
- Layer Six: Nation Union
- Layer Seven: World Union

LAYER ONE —
Internal Union

Genuine happiness and wellbeing is something that is felt on the inside, even if other people and situations are hugely important factors in our positive feelings. We are encouraged to be mindful, to manage our emotions in a positive way, to detach and accept life's challenges in ways that are not harmful to our equilibrium. Internal Union is a sense of inner peace, self-acceptance, and contentment. It's a state of mind that is free from anxieties, self-doubts, negative thoughts, and destructive emotions. In many ways, inner peace is connected to an ability to feel part of the whole. To see ourselves as one, not as separate from everyone else. It's a transcendental way of being.

This internal state of grace can be very difficult for humans, who have demanding egos and a need to compete, achieve, and survive. It is the same for your character. Inner peace means your character is not beating herself up about numerous things. She will look after herself, her needs, her health, and her security. She will know herself well, know her limits as well as her freedoms. She will feel confident, she will trust herself, she may even have conversations with herself. She will avoid guilt or self-blame for things that are outside her control. Maternal guilt will not be something she takes on.

Inner peace tends to be reflected in numerous ways in the physical self, not just through adornment, which can actually be a mask. The superficiality of the exterior doesn't exactly lend itself to a transcendental way of thinking. It can keep a character stuck. For some women, self-image anxiety is permanently in the back of their mind, to the point of obsession. Our culture celebrates and endorses narcissism, particularly in the young. To what extent your character is very confident and at peace with her physical self is worth exploring.

Self-Union also takes the form of masturbation. A woman who feels at one with herself can give herself pleasure in a very satisfying way. If she can't, then on some level she has an internal conflict nullifying her self-acceptance. This will be unique to the character.

LAYER TWO —
Significant Other

This layer is all about the sense of union we get from another individual. It's the governing principle behind the desire for love and intimacy. It symbolizes our need to find our soulmate — our friend for life and our fellow traveler. Union also reflects the earliest memories of oneness we all felt with our first carers, even the safety of the womb. Union, at its most primal, is a dependent and unconditional bond. Love with a significant other, whether it's a lover, a child, or a parent, can be blissful. It's nice to be completely understood, and to understand the other.

Women's desire for love is not necessarily stronger than men's, but it can dominate many female-driven stories. Female characters tend to express this desire more because it feels more permissible in many cultures. Emotionally expressive male protagonists, desperate for love and who reveal their vulnerability, certainly exist but are perhaps rarer.

The romantic ideal of man as savior is very powerful, but it can be an empty myth for women who have very close early relationships with both their mothers and fathers. These women have strong self-esteem, and idealization of men is not a big factor for them. If finding love is obsessing your heroine, it's a good idea to really know her backstory. What is getting in the way of her ability to find love with the right person? What wounds does she have to heal to be able to love? What capacity does she have for real love, as opposed to idealized love? How is she going to be loved, to be able to give love?

In love relationships, the physical act of sex, when it's between two people who really care for each other, is an intensely powerful union. Sex not based on intimacy tends to be fuelled by eroticism and fantasy projections about the other person. The sense of arousal is not based on knowing the person deeply, and doesn't have the sense of intimacy that comes from commitment, trust, and openness. This is why your character can have bad sex with the person she is committed to when trust issues and power dynamics are sabotaging the relationship. What kind of sex life does your heroine have? Think about how she feels pleasure, and whether intimacy is easy for her.

LAYER THREE —
Family

The Union in family life can be symbolized by birthdays, weddings, anniversaries, and even funerals. They are opportunities to share our deepest memories of the loved one, and perhaps bid them farewell. A family can give a sense of belonging and connection that is truly special and everlasting. Again, the biological family might not be as important as your character's "real" family — the people around her who really care for her. It's important for you to work out whether the family really offers her a sense of Union, and how. Does she feel like she belongs? Does the family validate and respect her? Do they offer unconditional love? Are they there when the going gets tough? What are the caring, positive values of the family?

Female friends and women's support networks become like family to many women. Women's ability to share and empathize with each other is equalized by their ability to care for each other. The notion of sisterhood is built on the belief that women understand the burdens placed on each other, and are the best people to really share the load. Caring sororities may be valuable to your character.

LAYER FOUR —
Community

Union is represented by all the ways a community looks out for its members, celebrating and supporting each other. To participate and belong, there needs to be give and take. Your character will always been in a community of one sort or another, so how is she going to experience Union there? Fetes, festivals, religious and spiritual centers, and community gardens are all examples of communities coming together to feel connected and promote good will.

LAYER FIVE —
Culture

Expressions of Union are shaped and determined by your character's culture. In the course of your research, you might find some surprising aspects of cultural Union. Whatever her culture, there will be a whole variety of ways that the expressions of union are permitted. Some societies have a problem with women smiling in public. Others believe female enjoyment of sex is wrong. In the West, some men expect women to smile and to appear amenable and subservient; heightening this lopsided power dynamic, these expectations are increasingly becoming normalized, even in situations where men and women are complete strangers. (The excellent *Everyday Sexism* blog has covered this topic in detail.) It can be an expectation and a demand for a *woman to please*, even if she doesn't feel like it.

LAYER SIX —
Nation

A nation's sense of Union is often seen in stories where success or achievement is celebrated collectively. This could be victory celebrations, Thanksgiving, coronations, or another kind of commemoration of national pride. Dedication is a strong drive in the female protagonist who wants to make her country proud or to fight for it in some way. National heroines can be sportswomen, warriors, leaders, politicians. They will derive satisfaction and respect from leading well. The truly heroic character who is not scared to put down her life is primarily motivated by the common good. If she survives, her victory is a shared one. Many women aren't recognized for their achievements until after their deaths, and remain forgotten heroines. Writing a film about their lives, to share it with the world, is a form of belated celebration.

LAYER SEVEN —
World

This Layer of Union is symbolized by the fragile notion of world peace. It comes from alliance and diplomatic efforts to sustain harmonious relations between countries. Women as politicians are taking their place on the world stage, yet there are still too few of them. The Olympics represent the global union of nations in sports. Although the action is competitive, the spirit of cooperation is the overriding principle. Women athletes extend female participation on the world stage.

⌒ EXERCISE ⌒
Union and Love

First, brainstorm all the Layers of Union in your female protagonist's world. As with the Layers of Conflict, if you are unsure, don't worry. This exercise is designed to trigger new insights.

Then, from your character's point of view, complete the Layers of Union Questionnaire on the next page.

Finally, if you are writing a story where an intimate relationship is explored, outline your story, identifying which Steps to Love function in your story.

⌒ Layers Of Union ⌒
QUESTIONNAIRE

1. What makes you happy? How do you show it? What do you love about yourself?
2. Are you in love?
3. Describe all the emotional aspects of your relationship that bring you joy.
4. Do you have a good sex life? What fulfills you sexually?
5. What's the best thing about your family?
6. Who are your best friends? Why do you love them?
7. Would you describe your local community as a happy one? Why?
8. Do you have children? What's the best bit about parenting for you?
9. Who or what do you love most in the world?
10. What is your happiest memory?

LAYERS OF UNION CASE STUDY:
Grace and Frankie

Grace and Frankie is a Netflix series that follows the growing friendship of two women in their seventies when their husbands, Sol and Robert, declare that they are gay, have been having a long-term affair, and want divorces from their wives. Grace and Frankie are forced by circumstance and their own fear of loneliness and redundancy into living together in Grace's beautiful beach house in La Jolla. The SuperTheme of *Grace and Frankie* is distinctly Feelgood and Familiar, showing two single, independent, glamorous, and passionate women living life on their own terms. The series totally subverts the stereotype of the lonely, sexually barren, bitter old woman who has no identity other that being a wife and grandmother. On the contrary, we follow the lives and loves in their senior years as they learn to rely on each other's support and make the most of the unexpected new lease on life they have been given.

Internal Union

Grace enjoys her image and looking good. She feels attractive and has a sense of poise, reflecting **an inner calm**. Grace **knows her own mind**, and speaks it. She is cool-headed when others are losing theirs. She refuses to stay in a relationship she doesn't feel meets her needs, owing to a **growing sense of self-awareness and self-esteem**. She enjoys her sense of irony. She likes to drink and **doesn't suffer guilt** about it.

Frankie relishes her ability to live a **passionate and spiritually evolved life**. She loves and **respects her body, and protects it from toxic substances**. She makes yam lube to enable her to have sex. Frankie feels **at one with the natural world** and environmental issues. She enjoys mind-altering natural highs, such as marijuana and Ayahuasca. She **meditates for inner peace**. She enjoys painting, including portraits of her vagina, reflecting **her high self-esteem**.

Significant Other
Grace gets over her hurt and betrayal of Robert quickly; she is honest that the marriage was dead. However, she **feels protective** of Robert when he has a heart attack. She knows and understands him, and **wants the best** for him. She learns to be sexually impulsive, and to **follow her own desires**. She gets enormous pleasure from an affair with her long-lost love, but feels **empathy** for his wife, who has Alzheimer's. She can **enjoy sex**.

Grace **generously shares** her beach house with Frankie. She values Frankie's understanding of her and the companionship she offers. She **enjoys the growing friendship** with Frankie, and **likes how her values are changing** as a result of the new relationship, and that Frankie is showing her new ways of being. She values the fact that she has a new best friend.

Frankie has an enduring love of Sol, her **best friend and soulmate**. She **respects his choices** in terms of sexuality. She isn't homophobic. She **embraces a new affair**, choosing an **emotionally and physically respectful** man whose values she shares.

Family and Friends
Grace is **warm** to both her daughters, and appreciates their awareness of how much she loves them, but she's not a hands-on or doting grandmother. She **is there for them** if they need her. She is dependable, but gives them space. She **appreciates and values the new possibilities** for her life, and is happy to move on. She hangs out with her old friends and accepts without rancor the fact that they have moved apart.

Frankie **adores her adopted sons**, to whom she is incredibly close. She and Sol have raised them to be **emotionally literate and to value their family traditions**.

Community

Grace learns to put herself out there, offering **mentoring and support** to disadvantaged young women. Her home is in a wonderful beach community in La Jolla.

Frankie gives ex-offenders art classes in the beach house. She is **nonjudgmental and supportive**. She has strong community contacts with organic farmers. She is a **community activist** who knows her rights.

Nation

Both Grace and Frankie live in an **exclusive, well-off** California beach community. They are well-provided for through the alimony from their wealthy lawyer ex-husbands. Their lives are comfortable, and they enjoy the **privileges of the wealthy**.

The Steps to Love

If you are developing a story that has the growth of an emotional relationship at its heart, it can be useful to have a model that helps you think through the dynamics that can be experienced as your character gets to know another person and forms a closer bond with them, wherever that may lead. Relationships are organic, constantly in flux, and sensitive to many internal and external factors. Many of the steps we take in love are truly repetitive, as well. Even when a couple is making progress, they might well repeat certain steps or experience more than one step simultaneously. A couple may go through the cycle and back to the beginning again. Or one person in the relationship might go back to earlier steps, or even jump ahead. This is commonly felt in relationships that seem out of balance, in which one person isn't ready for commitment or opening up and feels that the other is pushing too much. Just like the Phases of a story, these steps are not necessarily linear. Love goes back and forward as your character's circumstances, needs, and self-awareness evolve. She may get stuck at certain stages, unable to move on.

The Steps to Love model is inspired partly by Jungian feminist Clarissa Pinkola Estés's tale of the Skeleton Woman in her book *Women Who Run With the Wolves*, which she uses to describe the First Stages of Love. It's also inspired by our psychological patterns and dynamics, often involving defense mechanisms (especially projection), trust issues, and rejection complexes. In this way, it's a model of very loose stages that reflect the extremely fluid, backward-and-forward phases of falling in and out of love. Hopefully it feels resonant and relatable to anyone who has ever been in an intimate relationship! If you are building a love story, you might want to watch some love stories and see if any of the Steps are visible to you.

As you get to know the Steps to Love, you'll be able to use them to build the story you want to tell. In fact, the Steps to Love are completely complementary to the Phases. One set doesn't replace another, and you can pick and choose to suit the needs of your story. Remember, in love, we can stand on one step for a very long time. Or we can hop, skip, and jump in any order we feel like! Sometimes we tumble right back down and it takes a long time to pick ourselves up, let alone face the climb again.

Different films and genres reflect some of the steps and not others. It's common for romantic comedies to start with the first stage, "Rules of Attraction," and end with "Taking the Plunge," with the couple getting married. But increasingly, female-driven stories follow what happens after marriage or after divorce, or portray the dating game when participants have children or face other complications. The steps are no longer straightforward, because love never is. In fact, it is very common for a female-driven love story to focus on the way love relationships affect a character's sense of identity, as in the romantic drama *The Age of Adaline*. This story follows a female protagonist who is capable of deep love but avoids it because she will always outlive everyone she loves. The film tells us that great risk in love will be rewarded by great happiness.

You can also follow the Steps to Love in nonsexual relationships comprising two people with a very close bond. An example is the dramedy *Frances Ha*, which follows a young woman's lonely journey to developing the most important relationship of all: the one with herself. It reminds us that you can't love anyone else, or find someone who will love you well, until you know, accept, and love yourself.

The Steps are:

- Step One: The Void
- Step Two: Running Scared
- Step Three: Feeling the Fear
- Step Four: Killing Illusion
- Step Five: Baring the Soul
- Step Six: The Plunge
- Step Seven: Test of Trust
- Step Eight: The Lost Self
- Step Nine: Renegotiation
- Step Ten: Acceptance

STEP ONE —

The Void

Before a new relationship starts, there is usually some kind of void in a character's life. She may be single or unhappily married. She may have no need for a relationship, or she may crave one. She might have created a protective bubble around herself, or she might be on a dating frenzy. She might have survived the loss of a previous partner or other loved one. She might have stumbled into a professional relationship with the potential lover.

The Age of Adaline: Adaline, a woman who cannot age and hasn't aged since the 1950s, has existence down to a fine art. She lives alone; she changes identity often; she has elaborate ways of ensuring she is "off the grid" so no one can trace her. She has ways of experiencing long memories, sneaking peeks at old albums, and visiting places from her considerable past. The only ones who can get close to her are her daughter (now an elderly woman) and a long line of King Charles Cocker Spaniels.

Frances Ha: Frances experiences the Void after best friend Sophie distances herself from Frances by moving out of the apartment. Frances's life is empty and lonely. She doesn't know who she is. She desperately attempts to connect with other young people, but they always judge her as a misfit. She is alone in the world but doesn't want to admit this to herself.

STEP TWO —

Running Scared

The Heroine meets the potential lover and she ... runs scared! This is metaphoric, remember. She's not necessarily tearing off down the street. Attraction can be conscious or deeply unconscious, depending on where she is at in her life and what she is telling herself. She will normally trust her own intuition and projections about this potential lover, even if she hasn't yet realized that they could end up lovers. He or she might be exactly what the Heroine is looking for, or she might reel in horror at their odious traits. She might not feel that she is ready, and retreat. If she is desperate to love, she might be fearful that her new or potential lover might cause hurt or disappointment. He might not be interested, she might not be good enough, or he might be the same old bad type she is always attracted to. Unconscious feelings of inadequacy can dominate this time, with good and bad fantasies about the other person filling the mind. Defenses are huge and designed to protect both individuals. You can see this in countless romantic comedies in which both characters loathe the very aspects that they initially misread, but ultimately come to accept (and perhaps use to heal each other with). This reflects the dynamics of projection whereby another person reminds us of the parts of ourselves we don't like, but can't admit to.

One thing is for sure: Whatever information a heroine is telling herself about the other person, the last thing she knows is the truth about her potential lover. This can only be discovered by getting involved. Remember, the potential lover is also going through exactly the same kind of anxieties. Many relationships don't get to first base because one or the other takes off. A worst-case scenario is that a commitment, for whatever reason, is formed when the character is Running Scared. This could be because of an arranged marriage, or a character choosing to marry as a form of escape or because she has no other choice.

The Age of Adaline: Adaline meets Ellis on New Year's Eve. There is a strong attraction at first sight. She leaves the party before he can speak to her, but he catches up with her. She manages to dismiss him. Ellis is persistent, seeking Adaline out at the library where she volunteers.

Frances Ha: Frances runs scared from Sophie when she sees her at a drink reception at their old college. Frances does not want Sophie to see the extent of her failed loser life, since Sophie has moved on with her life. Frances also runs scared to Paris in a desperate attempt to be cool, to convince herself she can do successful things, but it all ends in failure, and she is again sad and alone. She is running scared from herself, a loser nobody wants to be with including herself.

STEP THREE —

Feeling the Fear

A deeper level of connection is achieved by new information, or a revelation about the potential lover, coming to light. He or she might ask the heroine on a date. She might ask him or her on a date. A heroine might have a one-night stand with the potential lover, and they could talk more openly afterward. There is a shift in perception about the other person, leading to both parties feeling that the risk of getting closer is worth taking. The unconscious dynamic behind this stage is that something about the other person reminds the heroine of herself, leading to a glimmer of empathy. The projections are still there, as the heroine is still largely defining the potential lover by her own experiences and assumptions. By opening the door slightly wider, the potential lover is let in a little bit more. Each partner feels the risk of proceeding is worth taking, even if it doesn't end up well and help the relationship go forward.

Age of Adaline: Adaline agrees to a date with Ellis, accepting dinner at his place and ending up in bed with him. She is allowing herself to let him in slightly, assuring herself that her protective safeguards are still in place. She is deluding herself since he is clearly the perfect man for her on every level.

Frances Ha: Trying to get over the loss of Sophie, Frances goes on a date with a boy that she likes. It doesn't go well; she is clumsy and gauche. She offers to pay, only to find that her card is rejected. She runs to an ATM and trips, hurting herself.

STEP FOUR —
Killing Illusion

If things do go well, the heroine wants to know everything about the lover. She is feeling deeply attracted, and wants to make sure she's making the right decision. In fact, the more they know, the more secure she will feel. Illusion only gets in the way of closeness. Depending on the intentions of the lover, he or she will feel the same. A deeper connection can grow from both lovers letting the mask down. The safer each person feels, the more truth they will reveal. Killing Illusion also involves confronting self-delusion. The defenses the heroine has built up around herself are exposed to the Self as a means of keeping others out. The loved one's baggage is recognized and accepted, and is not seen as a deterrent. Mutual opening up and surprising revelations can take place. Sometimes Killing Illusion does result in Running Scared by opening up a character who can't handle the truth. This can lead to a deep sense of betrayal in the other person, especially if sex has occurred. Killing Illusion can also take place during a separation. It reflects a deep need to know and to make sense of what went wrong, and what one's own part in it was.

The Age of Adaline: Adaline probes Ellis to find out if he is a playboy and/or attached. She wants to know what she is getting into with him. He is able to smash her illusions about him by being truthful and straight. He convinces her of his devotion to her.

Frances Ha: Much later, Sophie and Frances end up in bed together (platonically) after a drinks reception. Both girls open up to each other, and it is like old times. Frances realizes how messed up Sophie is, and how badly Sophie is treating her fiancé. The illusion of Sophie is finally crumbling.

Baring the Soul

Because Killing Illusion may have led to a relationship evolving, an even deeper layer of intimacy can be achieved. In stories, it is very common that Baring the Soul happens after a Test of Trust (see below), when one partner feels betrayed by the other. To save the relationship, the other has to put herself on the line and finally expose her vulnerability. Ideally, Baring the Soul leads to a true sense of intimacy that balances the relationship and makes both partners equal. It will lead to reciprocal trust and love. However, it's not impossible for a deeply damaged person to require the other party to Bare their Soul first to make them feel safe.

Baring the Soul is about reciprocity. It's the deepest form of transaction between two people. It's far more than just sex. The heroine now knows that her lover has the potential to heal her, and vice-versa. He or she has all the necessary qualities to make the heroine feel whole. Their love is complementary and healing. The feeling they are made for each other takes over at this stage. Feeling safe, the heroine faces up to her deepest inadequacies and projections. She feels an overwhelming need for her partner to know everything about her. She declares her deepest feelings and most private secrets, and puts herself on the line for love. She tells the lover how she feels about him and what she wants. This can result in passionate lovemaking as a form of communication, as both people physically open up to each other.

The Age of Adaline: Adaline bares her soul to her daughter, but only partially. She reveals that she cannot open her heart to romantic love with a man because the pain is too unbearable.

Feeling Good and Finding Love   177

She is fearful enough that she will eventually lose her daughter to old age and be truly alone. She later bares her soul to Ellis's father, whose heart she once broke. She tells him she cannot bear the pain of loss through separation and death, and that is why she is going to run away from Ellis.

Frances Ha: Frances is hurt because she bared her soul to Sophie, only to get rejected. Sophie knows her intimately, including her weaknesses and vulnerabilities. Dumped by Sophie, Frances almost bares her soul to her male friend Benji by seeking emotional support when she's low. It's a platonic relationship since they both consider themselves undateable. However, it is a positive step for needy and dependent Frances in terms of feeling less alone. She really needs to bare her soul to herself to know that unless she begins to depend on herself as much as she does other people, she will stay stuck and miserable.

STEP SIX —
The Plunge
The couple commit to being together and taking their love seriously. For adults, it can often come in the form of a marriage proposal, or a declaration of commitment. For teenagers, it is about getting serious and being seen as a couple by friends. A new era of love and coupledom has arrived, and there is no turning back. Feelings of idealization about an unconditional love can arise here. The couple looks forward to a life together. This doesn't mean that ghosts from the past can't re-emerge here in the form of old wounds being pressed. The happy ending of many romantic comedies shows the Plunge being taken.

The Age of Adaline: Adaline takes a Plunge in furthering the relationship by going on a date with Ellis. She shows him a secret part of the city, something he has never seen. She kisses

him and goes to bed with him, thinking she is in control —
but really she is falling headfirst in love with him, putting her
defense mechanisms in peril.

In *Frances Ha*, Frances needs to take the Plunge with
herself. She does so when she goes back to her old place of
work, but in administration, not dancing. The job gives Frances
financial stability so she can pursue her talent as a choreographer. She has made a commitment to herself.

STAGE SEVEN —
Test of Trust
The character's commitment is treasured or threatened here.
The Test of Trust can take the form of a wedding or a symbolic
union of the new life. Alternatively it can be the betrayal of
love. In a tragic love story, the Test of Trust can result in the
death or disappearance of a loved one. A sense of betrayal
can also happen here when an external factor exposes a
past secret.

The Age of Adaline: Adaline tests Ellis's trust in her by
turning nasty on him when he shows up at her place of work.
She feels violated by him, as he is breaking through her defense
mechanisms that keep emotional intimacy with men at arm's
length. Unable to be honest, she turns ugly, telling him it will
never work and that she is leaving. Later, she is retested by
being invited to Ellis's parents fortieth wedding-anniversary
weekend, only to discover that Ellis's father is none other than
a previous love of her life, someone who she ran away from
in the 1970s.

In *Frances Ha*, Sophie tests Frances's trust by moving out
of their apartment. Sophie kills illusion when she makes it
clear that she has other friends that are important to her. Later,
Frances finds out from other people that Sophie is engaged and

moving to Japan. Frances has to accept that she is relatively insignificant to Sophie now.

STAGE EIGHT —

The Lost Self

The committed relationship requires new compromises that all the stages up until the Plunge cannot fully prepare them for. It is as if, after the Test of Trust, the couple gives birth to a new collective identity that must be nurtured as well as their own individual selves. If the Test of Trust is failed, the character can feel lost and her identity shaken. She has to pick up the pieces of her shattered self, and move on. She can eventually re-enter the Void. However, the Lost Self can also indicate positive feelings in a heroine; she's lost sight of her true self, but doesn't believe this is important. She's so in love, nothing else matters. Countless heroines' love stories focus on the huge change of identity that a relationship can bring about.

The Age of Adaline: Ellis's father confronts Adaline with the truth about who she is, the woman he once loved. He recognizes her because of a scar on her hand that he himself stitched up in the 1970s. Adaline is devastated at being found out. She is unable to deal with the truth coming out; she has no sense of self to cope with it. She does not want to face the pain of loss. Adaline runs from Ellis, leaving a goodbye note. She hurtles away back to the city, back to another Void and a life alone, but this one tinged with intense heartbreak. She is running from a man who has the capacity to accept her, but she cannot bear the fact she will break his heart again one day, like she broke his father's.

Frances Ha: Most of the story is about Frances coming to terms with how lost she is, never having found her true identity. Her platonic love affair with Sophie was a catalyst for a journey to a stronger identity — but most importantly, it helped Hannah learn how to fall in love with herself. Frances lacked self-esteem and was lost long before Sophie came along, not having worked out how to define herself, an oddball in the tough and judgmental world of hip New York.

STAGE NINE —

The Renegotiation

The committed relationship is disrupted or challenged by internal or external factors. The equilibrium is disturbed by major events, such as the birth of children, infertility, or job and financial challenges, all of which put pressure on the relationship and necessitate a Renegotiation of the nature of the Union. Large-scale external factors such as war can threaten the love relationship. Internal needs and ambitions can threaten the couple's collective identity. One partner can feel left out or taken for granted. Old insecurities might resurface. Either partner has to go back to the steps of Killing Illusion or Baring the Soul to make the marriage or partnership survive; or it can be time to let the relationship die.

The Age of Adaline: When Ellis finds Adaline in the hospital, after her near-fatal car crash, she finally realizes that he simply must know the whole truth about her condition because of how much she deeply loves him. She kisses him passionately and begins her revelation about her bizarre syndrome of never aging. By being honest, they can start again.

Frances Ha: Frances needs to go back to work as a secretary, not a performer, in the dance company. She has to face and know her strengths as well as her weaknesses. She renegotiates a new way of being for herself. This means she has to let the past go, and bravely face a future relying on herself. She will only have a chance of a healthy relationship with another if she accepts herself and embraces the single life.

STAGE TEN —

Acceptance

The Renegotiation either results in a new form of Union, which is tolerance and acceptance of the other's relationship needs, or in the couple finding a way of dealing with external factors so they don't damage the relationship. There is a sense of acceptance that feels durable, of the relationship having been made stronger by having survived the challenge. Alternatively, the relationship will die, and both partners will re-enter the Void or experience the Lost Self (depending on how much the breakup affects them emotionally). In a long-term relationship, Acceptance can permeate the relationship on every level. Your heroine knows exactly how her partner ticks, and the compromise doesn't bother her. They have been through ups and down, trials and tribulations. Her partner is truly her other half.

The Age of Adaline: Adaline and Ellis move in together with her daughter. There are no secrets between the trio. Adaline doesn't have to run anymore, so can be loved and accepted for who she is; she can let a man in. Ellis will die one day, and she will outlive him, but it is better to have loved and lost than to always run scared. But then she sees a grey hair, and she realizes to her delight that she has been cured. She can age and die like a normal woman. Her acceptance has been rewarded by being cured.

In *Frances Ha*, Frances has to commit to herself and her dreams. She has to rent her own apartment and live alone. She has to put on a show, with her own team of dancers, which she has choreographed. She has to trust in her gifts and talents. She has to rely on nobody but herself, because she knows loving herself has given her true security. Frances finds acceptance of herself as a single woman with considerable creative talents. Her love for Sophie has been replaced by an increased ability to love and accept herself, to find self-worth through knowing herself better. She ends her story in a happy void with a potential date on the horizon. Because Frances is stronger as an individual, she will have a better chance of finding a healthy love.

Sex and Intimacy

Writing about sex may be something you really enjoy, or it can make you cringe. Whatever your attitude toward describing sexual intimacy and sexuality, you can't develop a fully functioning adult female protagonist without having at least considered this aspect of her being. Well, you could avoid it, but perhaps look at your own reasons for doing so. It doesn't matter if sex is in your story or not, your understanding of your protagonist could take on more dimensions if you explore her own unique ways of needing physical contact, and her own attitudes about sex and sexuality. These might be informed by the Maternal Lessons she received in the backstory, or how she identifies with the Lover Role-Choice. Your character's attitudes about sex may also be shaped by how she defines her sexuality, feels about herself and her body, decides who to trust and why, and internalizes or rejects the wider culture's values and expectations.

Intimacy-Embracing Female Protagonists:

- Like their own bodies
- Like making love
- Understand that emotional well-being influences sexuality
- Communicate through touch
- Enjoy the sensual as much as the sexual
- Rarely fake orgasms
- Assert their sexual needs

- Express desire
- Don't collude with sexual double standards (i.e., Don't believe in the concept of "the slut")

Intimacy-Avoidant Female Protagonists:

- May seek approval and self-worth from the sexual interest of men
- Feel uncomfortable expressing their needs
- Associate sex with loss of self-control
- Find sex embarrassing and shameful
- May have been abused
- May be influenced by ideological or religious conditions attached to specific ways of behaving sexually

Of course your character may experience both states of being at different times in her life, information presented in back-story or in the implications of her fate following the story's conclusion. The important issue to consider is how she relates on an intimate level, with whom, and why.

Sex on the Page

Sex, and how it functions in scripts, tends to be genre specific. The opening scene of the comedy *Bridesmaids* shows Annie having really bad sex and doing everything she can to please a guy; she keeps her needs to herself lest she bruise his ego or be seen as overly assertive (possibly a bit of both). The sex is shallow, energetic, and ultimately meaningless. It's just one of the many lies Annie tells herself to counter her sense of personal failure. Annie is an intimacy-avoidant *female protagonist* at this stage of her journey. She is not capable of expressing her needs. She lets herself be used, and functions like a sexual plaything.

You may opt to write "they f**k" in your script, or "they make love," depending on your tone — or you may wish to go into vivid action prose. The scene from *Bridesmaids* is written in such a way that the comedy escalates, leading to an "anti-climax" for Annie when she is unceremoniously asked to leave by her clearly disinterested lover. The sex itself is ridiculous and funny, full of physical comedy as the couple copulate vigorously on the bed. Annie's emotions aren't so funny. The juxtaposition shows us just how far she has to travel emotionally on her journey to self-respect, and we are only on page 1!

CHAPTER 7

Writing the Female-Driven Biopic

A s fictional biopics, true stories about women's lives and achievements are enormously popular and seem to be on the rise. A known or little-known character can be an appealing and commercial proposition in that she is already a "brand" — the audience and the interest are already there. As a writer of a screenplay about a real woman, there can be some useful creative strategies to consider when choosing and building the story of her life, achievements, and notoriety. See them as a set of suggestions that may help you streamline your passion and enthusiasm for what is probably an exceptional female character.

A Passionate Inspiration

Often, you are attracted to a real woman's life because of what she managed to achieve against all obstacles, the main one normally being her gender. The second appealing factor could be the actual nature of The Achievement, a term that covers a range of reasons why the person is known more widely — including a triumph, a skill, a crime, a birth "right" such as royalty or aristocracy, or a long and glittering career. It broadly covers what she is famous for.

As a biopic writer, you strongly relate to The Achievement, or find it spectacularly interesting or inspirational. For instance, you might love the life of royal women or a certain period of history. A common third factor is an emotional connection with your subject. Maybe you can relate to what she went through, or you feel you understand her approach to her work or achievement on a deep level. Maybe the particular barriers she faced are key to your connection with her. She is a role model for you, someone you look up to.

Other, less obvious motivations to create a biopic about a particular person's life include:

Celebrating the unknown/known life

You are motivated to share this woman's experiences with the wider world because you feel she is worthy of attention due to The Achievement. You may feel she has been wrongfully overlooked by history, or that she has been somehow neglected. Otherwise you may feel that the common perception of her is somehow wrong, that somehow she has been misrepresented or her personality distorted, and you want to put things right.

Conscious representation of gender roles in a true life

You want to focus on the gender constraints she suffered. Maybe she was the first woman to ever do something. Maybe she had to face a derisive, threatened, or hostile "patriarchy." Maybe her obstacles were so huge, it's simply amazing she managed to achieve anything.

Avoidance/subversion of cliché or stereotype of a known woman

You think there are clichéd representations about your subject, or this type of woman, or somehow she's been treated in a stereotypical way. You want to subvert these by showing other sides of her personality or aspects of her work that the public wouldn't necessarily know.

Avoidance of relationship-oriented stories

You want to focus purely on the struggle of The Achievement. You are fed up that when it comes to female-driven biopics, her personal relationships are almost as important as her triumph or achievement. You may feel there's a sexual double standard at work when it comes to true-life female protagonists, which renders them noteworthy for their relationships as much as their important Achievement. You also believe that many women of achievement didn't actually put emotional relationships first in their real lives. To make them likable or relatable, you feel their relationships are always given too much story.

Embracing relationship-oriented stories

Conversely, you are fascinated by the emotional world of your subject because you feel that women are conditioned to please other people and meet others' needs before their own. You may like exploring divided loyalties and the impact of love on your protagonist, who had a big challenge or quest. Even if she had to repress the nurturing and relating side of herself, you feel that makes her relatable, credible, and interesting to audiences.

No restrictions on narrative territory

You like the fact that you can use historical fact to determine your plot. The challenge to create a dramatic story through facts is compelling to you. You particularly like the fact that you can show a woman doing or being something amazing, and you don't have to "prove" that she is credible. Because she is real, and did it, there's no argument! Perhaps if she were fictional, nobody would believe her!

Genre breaking

You'd like to write a biopic in an unexpected genre, not just a heavy drama. You're inspired by biopics that have comic touches or surrealism. You want to mix things up a bit in the storytelling.

Reaching an underserved audience

Your biopic will tell the story of someone who may not be particularly well known to the wider world, but she is very well known to experts or those who work in her field. In this way you have a readymade audience, something that can only foster support for your project.

A new vision

You know there are many versions of your subject's life. But you are burning to bring something new and unknown to the party!

Handling The Achievement

Now you need to think about what you want to focus on in your story in terms of The Achievement. Remember, this is a broad-spectrum term.

The way you approach The Achievement is a "governing principle" of your story.

You need to remember that most biopics involve several of the following approaches to The Achievement. Too many, and your story could be a little cluttered. That might not be a problem if you like big and blousy biopics!

The Whole Life (or the vast majority)

Do you want to celebrate the entire life of the subject in your story? (e.g., *La Vie en Rose*, *Frida*, *The Iron Lady*) The "whole life" approach to The Achievement can involve a complex linear structure, with interweaving storylines at different stages of the subject's life. Your main motivation is to explore and celebrate her lifelong experiences with the subject, sometimes so that you can reveal key themes of her life.

If you like epic-style biopics, which span a whole lifetime and which show the growth and evolution of a character, this approach to The Achievement may appeal to you.

The Big Romance

This approach tends to relegate The Achievement, or at least put it in the context of the emotional life of the subject. In female-driven biopics, it is frequently combined with other approaches to The Achievement. You may find a grand passion or secret dalliance that is fascinating or even little known. This approach to The Achievement doesn't have to negate the achievement, but it capitalizes on the fact that the audience knows this subject, and therefore should be interested in their personal life! Perhaps the impossibility of love, or the love that is sacrificed so that the character can go onto The Achievement, is what you want to explore. (e.g., *My Week With Marilyn*, *Becoming Jane*) The Big Romance can make a little-known person very well known (e.g., *The Invisible Woman*) because of their association with the subject.

If you are interested in strongly emotional stories where love is both a catalyst yet something to be sacrificed for a wider goal or greater good, this approach to The Achievement is probably very interesting to you.

The Little-Known Angle

Perhaps you've found an odd episode or incident in the known subject's life that shows them in a new light. It could cover a very short time scale. Unfortunately, female-driven biopics don't tend to use this approach to the Achievement as frequently as male-driven biopics, such as *Frost/Nixon*, do. This may be due the fact that female-driven biopics are still more relationship-oriented, as mentioned below. However, one example is *Coco Before Chanel*, which is also blended with The Big Romance.

The Main Event/Achievement

This approach to The Achievement puts it center stage. The main character's pursuit and/or experience achieving what they are most widely known for, or the identity they have sought, is followed. The obstacles and the tenacity of the main character as she goes about the achievement form the central spine. (e.g., *Marie Antoinette, Big Eyes, The Lady, Wild*)

If you are fascinated by what your subject is actually known for, this is probably a good approach to The Achievement for you as you can really go into depth regarding the subject's journey to achieving her goal — and celebrate her triumph.

Breeding of a Monster

Perhaps your subject had a dysfunctional personality or difficult or deep character flaws and you want to illuminate these aspects, and the factors that caused them, perhaps in connection with tragedy in her life. It could be addiction, mental illness, or alienating behaviors that result in her falling afoul of the system or people. You may also want to consider the extent to which being difficult contributed to her success or notoriety. (e.g., *Monster, Factory Girl, Mrs. Parker and the Vicious Circle*)

This approach takes careful handling regarding your "feminist" intentions in celebrating a subject's life. Are you being gratuitous, or is an unconscious misogyny driving you? Are you allowing her to triumph despite her character flaws, or does she end up lonely and tragic? A good male-driven biopic to consider is *The Aviator* (utilizing the Whole Life/Breeding of a Monster approaches), in which the character of Howard Hughes is portrayed in context to his obsessive-compulsive and agoraphobic disorders, yet also triumphs at the end. Alternatively, do you believe that difficult women who achieve things are more interesting than difficult men because they defied expectations?

An Interesting Phase

Where the Little-Known Angle focuses on a specific and unknown event or situation, this covers a period of your character's life where she tries to become somebody else or she experiences a new stage of life beyond The Achievement. Alternatively the phase could show part of her life before she was famous or involved in her work. It could focus on some of the obstacles or relationships that shaped the main character and formed a foundation to her future path. (e.g., *Coco Before Chanel*, *Iris*, *Grace of Monaco*, *An Education*)

Finding the Biopic Emotional Engine (BEE)

When you have worked out which structuring approach to the Achievement inspires you and somehow feels right, now you need to think about an emotional journey that fits and supports your approach. The right Biopic Emotional Engine will support your themes, and what you really want to say about this woman's identity, personality, and life.

A *Biopic Emotional Engine* defines the protagonist's feelings about herself and her achievement

Each Biopic Emotional Engine can be seen as the powerful inner drive compelling your character, whichever one you choose. It's a good idea to try to choose the right BEE early — but don't worry if you can't. Very often, one will leap out at you from the start. Sometimes several BEEs may work well together.

The BEES are:

* Path to Wholeness
* Tests of Love
* Group Endeavor
* Quest
* Survival
* The Wandering Woman
* Rites of Passage

Let's have a look at each one.

Path to Wholeness

This BEE is often featured in the Whole Life or the Big Romance approaches. The protagonist feels emotionally incomplete or wounded to the point that her identity is fragmented and she needs to find inner equilibrium by healing these wounds. She might be completely abused or mentally ill. She could be recovering from illness. She might feel totally betrayed or let down by love, so she badly needs to recover. Her emotional story focuses on her experience of becoming whole, or trying to become whole with the help of others. Examples include: *Bessie, Saving Mr. Banks, Wild, Brooklyn,* and *The Iron Lady.*

Tests of Love

Normally found on the Big Romance, this BEE is taken by the protagonist as she becomes increasingly absorbed by the relationship with her significant other, and her emotions are somewhat governed by the dynamics between them. Intense romantic or platonic love might get in the way of her achievement, or they might propel her further in her field, like a rebound. Love can be both a help and/or a hindrance. Her feelings can generate conflicts in love including obsessional neediness, acute loneliness due to pining for the beloved, her own unresolved fear of abandonment, actual abandonment, and feeling trapped, controlled, or undermined by a lover. The love may not be romantic, but could be parental, or the love of best friends or working partners. Examples include: *Big Eyes*, *The Invisible Woman*, and *The Danish Girl*.

Group Endeavor

A couple or several protagonists are involved in an Achievement, and this BEE focuses on the group dynamics. They may depend deeply on each other or live together as a community. Solidarity and divisive behaviors within the group are often focused on in female-driven Group Endeavors. The ensemble also faces numerous patriarchal or misogynistic obstacles that bond them or divide them. They may have an experience together in which they discover new aspects and deeper feelings about each other. Loyalty, shared history, celebration, and togetherness are features of each character's journey. Each individual, however, may be driven by their own BEE. Examples include: *Calendar Girls*, *Made in Dagenham*, and *Suffragette*.

Quest

The protagonist is single-minded and gives herself a quest or mission; or she is given one by an external factor or person and she accepts it, perhaps with ambivalence or dread. This BEE reflects her determination and dedication to the Achievement. As she spends her time pursuing the quest, it becomes the significant other in her life, dominating all her thoughts. Loved ones get pushed back. Allies are those who share interest in the quest. The quest may change her, making her grow or (rarely) shrink in reaction to the challenge. The Main Event and a Little-Known Angle approaches to the Achievement often take this form. Quests can range from running a zoo in *We Bought a Zoo* to hiking the Pacific Coast Trail in *Wild* to finding out the truth about a son's disappearance in *Philomena*. Other examples include *Erin Brockovich* and *The Iron Lady*.

Survival

The subject's life, or those of the people she loves, is under threat, creating fear and a need to protect and survive. All her energies and emotions revolve around staying alive and outwitting or defeating the forces of destruction. Often her drive to protect herself and the rights of others are very entwined, leading to conflicts of interest. Survival can include emotional survival when her whole identity is being savaged by another person. Examples include: *Elizabeth*, *Erin Brockovich*, *The Lady*, *Precious*, and *Suffragette*.

Wandering Woman

The subject needs to keep moving. She's essentially restless, nomadic, or naturally an outsider. Her story just might be another stop along the way of her life. She might have found herself stuck and needs to move on, but can't. Frequently an Outsider or Incomplete Heroine, the female protagonist finds difficulty in belonging or finding herself. She may journey with others, or alone, and this may cause conflict. The big questions are where and how will she settle? Is she able to change sufficiently to belong somewhere? Sometimes she might not be aware that she needs to heal in order to learn to stay put, but her eyes might be opened to other needs as she travels. (e.g., *Hideous Kinky*, *Wild*)

Rites of Passage

The protagonist is dealing with a major transition that propels her into a new stage of life. These can be pregnancy, having an abortion, becoming a mother, having empty-nest syndrome, becoming a stepmother, losing a child, getting married, getting divorced, becoming a grandmother, going through menopause, or getting Alzheimer's. This BEE is firmly focused on identity issues affecting the subject. The factors that trigger the rites of passage, the people who support her through it, and the ways she feels about herself and her life are frequent features of this journey. (e.g., *Elizabeth: The Golden Age*, *Iris*)

The Talent

The protagonist has a Talent that is central to her sense of identity. It feels innate to her. She's really good at something, to the point of perfection and mastery. It is usually what she is known for. In pursuing her Talent, the heroine encounters many different experiences and obstacles. Sometimes it can seem that the Talent may actually destroy her, as it dominates her. Conflicts tend to be internal, as she is gripped by the need to express the Talent. But the Talent consumes her; she can't give it up without losing a sense of identity and purpose. The Talent emphasizes the domination of this gift over the protagonist's identity. *Frida*, *La Vie en Rose*, *Bessie*, *Amelia*, and *Joy* are all examples of the Talent.

Character-Development Dilemmas

In the course of your research you may encounter some dilemmas as you build your character. There are no easy solutions for any of these dilemmas, but one guiding principle is staying true to your own interpretation of who the female protagonist is, what she represents to you, and why you want to tell this version of events.

Regret — Many female protagonist-driven biopics focus on the high personal cost the Achievement has on the subject by jeopardizing love, relationships, or obligations to others so she may follow her dreams. This isn't as much of an issue with male biopics. Your reasons as a writer for focusing on these personal costs may include a belief that it is tougher for women to follow their dreams because of societal expectations that they put other people first, particularly their children. Maternal guilt, you may feel, is a valid theme since your subject must have encountered guilty feelings and terrible conflicts during her Achievement. Other reasons may include a fear of alienating the audience, or wanting to dispel a common belief that the subject was ruthless. An extreme example is when the female protagonist of a biopic is being tortured in old age by the memory of abandoning children or not having any. Regret can also include romances that somehow didn't stay the course, for which the subject feels responsible in some way.

Guilt, regret, self-destructiveness, and love and loss do seem to be recurring and poignant issues in the female biopic. If these are relevant to your subject, ask yourself if it is the right focus and why you are more interested in these issues than the challenge or triumph of the Achievement for its own sake. Women are often portrayed as sad, lonely, and alone (and even dead!) despite their considerable Achievements. These become big features of the story. What does this imply for you?

Not liking the character — We don't always like our characters. You might find yourself applying value judgments to your character, particularly if she was abandoned. Are you being influenced by an unconscious sexual double standard?

Your impression/everybody else's impression — Famous people are a little like brands in that everybody relates to what they symbolize in individual ways. What Virginia Woolf means to one person might not be the same as what she means to another. You may never have heard of her if you are a millennial! She might just be a name in a play to you. The point is your re-creation of the subject may be difficult for those who have a completely different attitude and interpretation of their life and what they mean. We all project onto famous/infamous people those qualities and traits that we want them to stand for. Likewise, not everybody knows all the same facts about the subject.

Somebody Else's Life, Somebody Else's Work

At all times remember that ethical and legal issues and permissions concerning the character that you are researching and creating, whether they are dead or alive, will require expert advice. This also applies if you are using other people's research on your subject. Laws about copyright and life rights and permissions vary from country to country, and it is your responsibility to do your research before you write a biopic.

Biopic Case Study 1:
Bessie

Bessie is a biopic about Bessie Smith that follows Bessie as she rises from difficult and humble origins to stardom as Queen of the Blues; the story focuses on her closest relationships as well as her professional endeavors, creating a memorable portrait of an ambitious, magnetic, and wounded character.

Bessie Smith is known for her incredible voice and raw blues that symbolize an era. The Achievement in *Bessie* is presented as the *Main Event*; Bessie's singing ambitions, and the highs and lows of her career, dominate the story, as does the *Big Romance* — in Bessie's case, several romances. The key moments of her love affairs are entwined, exploring the close resonance between Bessie's lyrics and the turbulence in her life. The plot is linear, but is broken up by flashbacks that reveal Bessie's biggest wounds: the loss of her mother and subsequent tough childhood at the hands of her sister Viola.

The Biopic Emotional Engines in *Bessie* are:

The Talent: *Bessie* gives a harrowing portrait of the struggles to stardom for a young black female singer in the racist Deep South of the 1920s and 1930s. An Incomplete Heroine due to deep emotional wounds, not only does Bessie have to contend with poverty and lack of contacts for an aspiring singer, she has a dearth of confidence evidenced by her rather flat stage presence. She is even too dark-skinned for some black-owned nightclubs and their promoters; the pay is miserable; the odds seem stacked against Bessie getting anywhere. She also hasn't been trained how to sing and perform. Her clothes reflect both her penury and her tough life. But Bessie has self-belief and an undeniable talent. She also wants to be special, to be watched, to have an audience. Bessie craves attention, and the chance to sing.

It is not until she sees the brilliant Ma Rainey perform that she takes the plunge and persuades Ma to let her join her traveling revue. Ma is the first supportive mentor to help Bessie develop as an artist. Bessie learns to project herself, and gains confidence on stage. Her voice is stronger than Ma's, and she is soon getting more attention and applause on stage. Loving the appreciation, Bessie's ambition results in her not caring that she is outshining Ma on stage; feeling annoyed that her protégé's ego results in a lack of respect for her, Ma sacks Bessie.

Bessie continues to rise with the support of her brother Clarence. Bessie's ascent is partly helped by Jack Gee, her violent husband, who lands Bessie a recording deal. He gradually takes over her affairs, causing Bessie to question matters, but she is not entirely comfortable challenging him. Fame gives Bessie a mixed life: she's got the fancy clothes, the money, the shows, the recording deal, the entourage, even her own train like Ma Rainey; she travels around the Deep South giving big tent shows. But her loneliness and alcoholism increase. After an emotional breakdown, Bessie begins to pick up the pieces of her career, returning at a more modest level. John Hammond, who respects and treasures her talent, approaches her; he provides the backing and support for her comeback tour.

Path to Wholeness: Bessie carries a deep, unresolved wound caused by the death of her mother. She is tortured by a childhood memory of the emotional and physical abuse dished out by her sister Viola, who cruelly threatened her after the death of her mother. Bessie hasn't been able to face the grave of her mother. Her wounds eventually contribute to her heavy drinking and codependency in a volatile relationship with Jack Gee that is plagued by infidelity, fights, alcoholism, and abuse. But Bessie is not a helpless victim. She has strong character traits: a sense of empowerment and the need for self-determination. Attacked, she will fight back.

When a man she is kissing doesn't understand "no," she attacks him. Similarly, she refuses to be put in her place by Ma Rainey. Equally, she doesn't like anyone intimidating her or her people. Heroically and fearlessly, she stands up to the very intimidating Ku Klux Klan, who are threatening to burn down her big tent show; bravely, Bessie sees them off. Jack Gee is the one person who manages to control and undermine Bessie's self-determination. Loving Jack and scared of abandonment, she gives him too much power. He becomes rich and successful on the back of her talent and hard work; he is a skilled predator and emotional manipulator. She creates a family home for her relatives, an opulent, big house. Jack's male ego is bruised. He turns to younger, "prettier" women, using Bessie's money to push another singer's career.

The pain, use, and abuse are too much for Bessie, and she hits the bottle. After Jack Gee kidnaps their son and leaves for another woman, blaming her drinking and justified that he made the money as much as she did, Bessie is devastated. The Depression wipes out her resources. Bessie crashes, losing her home, leading to an emotional breakdown. Critically, she stops singing and performing. It is the love and support of her brother Clarence, who never leaves her, and of Ma Rainey, who takes Bessie in when she is at her lowest, which help Bessie during the dark times. As Bessie's Path to Wholeness gets stronger, she turns to her lover Richard for an equal and caring relationship. He is with her when she visits her mother's grave, indicating closure on her worst nightmare. The story ends with Bessie feeling strong and positive, looking forward to the future. She is whole, and she has triumphed.

Tests of Love: Bessie is never alone and has a series of passionate relationships that range from the good to the completely dysfunctional. She needs people around her to compensate for her inner loneliness. Her main love affairs are with Lucille, a young woman who travels with her; Jack Gee, her husband/manager; and finally Richard Morgan, her bootlegger. Bessie loves too much, and expects people to be unconditionally loyal and loving.

BIOPIC CASE STUDY 2:
Saving Mr. Banks

P.L. Travers is the author of the Mary Poppins series of books. *Saving Mr. Banks* follows Pamela Travers, or "Mrs. Travers" as she prefers to be named, as she reluctantly goes to Hollywood to develop her world-famous *Mary Poppins* children's book into a screenplay for Walt Disney. There, she encounters her worst fears in the adaptation plans of the American creative team. Travers becomes increasingly hostile, rude, and rigid, treating her collaborators with no respect, making the collaborative process hell with her disdain and lack of compromise. Travers's resistance and negativity flummox Disney, a man used to getting his way. Sensing it has to do with her family, he tries to get through to her, but to no avail. Travers deeply needs to protect the character of Mr. Banks, whose plight is clearly inspired by her father, a creative, childlike soul who hated working in banks.

Feeling tricked and compromised, Travers finally erupts, leaving L.A. without assigning the rights to her book. She is surprised when Disney follows her to London. She finally relents when Disney reaches out, assuring her that he loves the story and the characters, and that they are safe with him, particularly the character of Mr. Banks, who embodies many of Travers's feelings about her own father. A parallel, interweaving storyline reveals Travers's turbulent childhood in Australia, as a little girl nicknamed Ginty, where her beloved but damaged father becomes increasingly alcoholic and wretched before finally dying young of tuberculosis. Ginty rages at the aunt who arrives, Mary Poppins–like, to save the desperate family, but who fails to rescue her father; this is the deepest reason why Mr. Banks has to be saved in the book and the film.

The Achievement is presented in the form of an "Interesting Phase" — the relatively short period of time when Travers goes to L.A. at the behest of Walt Disney. The adaptation of a novel provides the main plot; on the surface, it's not the most dramatic of situations for a feature film. However, the Interesting Phase in *Saving Mr. Banks* provides a fascinating glimpse at the deeper emotional drives behind a writer's creative processes and the emotional investment in, and attachment to, one's work. It charts the painful process of letting go that writers undergo if their work is going to reach the screen. The Interesting Phase also includes a poignant father/daughter love story that is utterly tragic, but linked to the main story through the emotional world the female character carries.

The Biopic Emotional Engines are:

Quest: Travers is reluctant to go on the mission to adapt her book, and she stays reluctant right to the end. The motivating factor is that she wants to keep her house, and now that royalties from the book have dwindled, she is broke and has nothing to live off. The task takes on greater and greater significance on a deeply emotional level. Her attitude is one of hate and snobbery, of Los Angeles, Disneyland, American food, American customs; she's even shockingly rude and ungrateful to Walt himself. Unreachable, she is utterly lonely the whole time, only slowly opening up to her driver. As the good-natured creative team tries their best to make Travers see the possibilities of the adaptation, through music, songs, and images, she increasingly tightens her grip on the story, becoming more hostile to the process. Even the money doesn't change her mind because she blames it for destroying her father.

Tests of Love: The young Ginty, an imaginative and happy child, loves her father with all her heart. He is a kind, adoring father with a magical imagination who plays games with Ginty, his favorite child, and promises never to lose her. Her love for him makes the unbearable bearable: the loss of the family home as her father gets sacked yet again, a move to the Australian outback away from smart Melbourne, the misery of her ground-down and deeply depressed mother. Yet again, Travers the father cannot cope with his job and is nearly fired. He embarrasses himself publicly being drunk, humiliating himself and his family. Sick with TB he takes to bed, too weak. When Ginty tries to find him drink, her idolized father turns on her angrily. He asks her to buy him pears, but by the time she gets back, he has died. Ginty feels she has failed him. She suffers the loss of her father and the loss of hope in others. Nobody could save him and this permanently wounds the young Ginty.

~~~~~~~~~~~~~~~~~

CHAPTER 8

Creating TV Female Protagonists:
Finding the Metaphoric Wound

We are living in the golden age of television, and gracing our screens are innumerable fantastic female characters as protagonists, secondary characters, antagonists, and returning characters. If you watch a lot of television, you will have your favorite shows. Perhaps it's the genre that grabs you; perhaps it's the lead character. A lot of people claimed not to be the biggest fan of fantasy until *Game of Thrones* came along. Ditto legal dramas until *The Good Wife* appeared. The formats and genres of TV are enormously diverse, but annual statistics show that male characters still outnumber female characters and are more diverse in occupation and age.

If you want to develop and pitch a female-driven television series, your biggest challenge will be creating distinctive and original main characters who can go the distance and remain fresh throughout television's long-running seasons (unless you have a miniseries in mind). This is where gender can help, because a female protagonist can open up perspectives that can still feel fresh and original and push the boundaries of the genre. In ensembles, with a number of supporting female characters, this can also be the case. This can be due to any of the following factors, or a combination thereof:

- The protagonist remains something of the Outsider Heroine; she doesn't exactly belong to the world and is different somehow, and part of her journey is to make sense of who she is and how she can find a place in the world. *The Good Wife, Orange Is the New Black, Veronica Mars.*

- Being female, she's in a world where she strongly identifies with competing Role-Choices. How does she negotiate "feminine" Role-Choices with "masculine" Role-Choices? (The most classic example is being a mom and simultaneously having a successful career.) *Veep, The Good Wife, Madam Secretary, Scandal, The Honourable Woman.*

- She's distinctive because of her age, ethnicity, sexuality, ability, and her M-Factor. She represents diversity AND has an M-Factor; we just haven't seen a female protagonist like her lead a series. *How to Get Away With Murder, Scandal, House of Cards, The Bridge, Homeland, Olive Kitteridge.*

- She's showing us a new and special world or experience, one that we have never seen before through the eyes of someone like her. *Penny Dreadful, Supergirl, Jessica Jones, Agent Carter.*

- She's exploring her relationships with women in fresh and original ways. *Girls, Mom, Broad City, Call the Midwife, Grace and Frankie.*

- She's exploring her relationships with men in fresh and original ways. *The Blacklist, The Fall, New Girl, Girls.*

TV Genres, Gender Awareness, and Role-Choices

The female character has come into her own on TV because her presence pushes the boundaries of many TV genres; by having a main female character in traditionally male-dominated genres, shows have become more feminist and more "feminized," as male and female characters subvert gender expectations. "Masculine" female characters are avoiding relationships, getting older, becoming cynical loners. "Feminine" male heroes, such as Don Draper in *Mad Men*, are on "heroine's journeys" as much as they are on "hero's journeys," and are finding their true selves beyond the gender expectations of their time.

Using Role-Choices in developing your TV-series protagonist and cast of characters can be an effective way of ensuring diversity. Questioning your bias about certain genders is relevant when you have a cast much bigger than that in a feature film. You need to work harder at making sure your female characters don't all identify with similar Role-Choices; ditto your male characters. Working on the unique memorability of each character becomes vital. In your crime series, are the victims predominantly female? Are the criminal masterminds (the bad Bosses) always male? Who is doing the nurturing? Who is doing the seducing? Who is having more fun? Which sex are you allowing to be dark, dangerous, and triumphant? In terms of cast design, supporting characters also need to be diverse, original, and willing to stand their own ground.

Let's see how dominant Role-Choices can be used in mapping out roles with main characters in two popular TV genres.

Zombie Apocalypse:
The Walking Dead

Rick: Hero, Heroine, Lover, Father, Mother, Warrior, Boss, Lover, Rival.
Michonne: Hero, Heroine, Lover, Mother, Warrior, Victim.
Carol: Warrior, Mother, Victim, Hero, Heroine, Wife, Rebel.
Daryl: Rebel, Child, Warrior, Victim, Mother, Hero, Heroine.

Everyone is a **Victim** in *The Walking Dead* because they have endured great loss: of loved ones, of identity, of their whole life as they knew it. Surrounded by "walkers," the millions of zombies, everyone is a potential literal Victim, almost every minute of every day if they let their guard down. In the new society, where new tribes, rules, and social order slowly emerge, both males and females have a chance at equality. The Role-Choices that Rick and Michonne identify with reflect this equality. Rick is **Boss**, but he is taking over from Deanna, a woman. Likewise, most characters identify with the **Warrior**, a fearless fighter. They need to fight and kill to survive/displace enemies and other threats. Each character has highly individual "rites of passage": their experiences becoming Warriors and the moral issues they face as killers. They all need to kill to protect themselves and each other, but how comfortable they are with this new identity ranges hugely from character to character.

Each episode, the main characters have a quest identifying them with the **Hero** Role-Choice. They have a goal, motivated by the greater needs of the tribe. They need to gather food, water, and health supplies; defend their home; kill zombies; and chase off/escape from rivals and enemies. But at the same time, their search for a meaningful identity puts them all on Heroine's Journeys. As **Heroines**, they are working out who they are, where they fit, what morality means to them in the new world, and how they want to be defined in relationship to others.

Mother is the Role-Choice associated with the human need for nurturing: all the characters here show mothering to the vulnerable, to the surviving and newborn children, and to each other. They work at bringing nurturing into the family/tribe. For those who have lost children, becoming symbolic Mothers again while undertaking the necessary killing they have to do as Warriors can be a painful dual role. The loss of the old self, from pre-zombie times, and the memories of failing to protect children prove to be incredibly painful. The Mother, motivated to care, nurture, and simply be there, makes them human rather than dehumanized Warriors. Their romances associate them with the Role-Choice of **Lovers**, each character expressing this in individual ways. Maggie and Glenn are deeply in love and want to create a family. Michonne and Rick's love grows out of mutual respect, trust, and bonding. Carol's soulmate would appear to be Daryl, but this doesn't become romance.

FAMILY SITCOM:
Mom

Christy — Child, Victim, Mother, Father, Caryatid
Bonnie — Mother, Rebel, Lover, Child, Amazon, Victim
Marjorie — Healer, Mother, Lover
Violet — Child, Wife, Mother, Lover

Mom follows the intense love/hate dynamics between single mother Christy and her mom Bonnie, who was also a single mom when she had Christy. Christy is trying to turn her life around and be a functional mother to her kids, Violet and Roscoe, when Bonnie moves in. Bonnie is an irreverent free spirit, not as far along as Christy in overcoming addiction and her resolution to change. The **Mother** Role-Choice is central as both Christy and Bonnie try desperately to break destructive patterns to be functional moms. Living together generates huge conflict between mother and daughter, as well as opportunities for resolution and healing in the mother/daughter relationship.

When Christy's daughter Violet gets pregnant very young, it appears that the single-mother pattern is repeating itself all over again, something very scary for Christy. However, Violet bravely breaks the pattern and gives the baby up for adoption. Both Bonnie and Christy are former addicts; they have had bad spells of acute alcohol addiction and both are now in the same AA group. Their AA friends, including Marjorie, form a supportive **Sorority**, characterized by empathy, tough talk, and looking out for each other, particularly when sobriety is threatened. The AA group also functions as a symbolic **Healer**. The strongest and wisest member of the group, Marjorie, suffers from breast cancer and is a wounded Healer. Marjorie is stable and sensible, with a "crazy cat lady" side. She is a symbolic Mother to Christy, who instinctively trusts her more than Bonnie.

Bonnie still identifies as a **Rebel** — angry, defiant, irreverent, and impulsive. These traits repeatedly get her into trouble, and not only with Christy. She is the first of the two to relapse. Conversely, Christy empowers herself to study law, indicating an identification with the responsible **Caryatid**.

Both mother and daughter are prior **Victims** of their addiction, something that destroyed both their lives in the past. When Bonnie relapses, she is a victim of her own weakness. Society has given them little opportunity to improve their hard-luck situations.

The **Lover** Role-Choice is reflected differently in each woman. Christy avoids intimacy due to low self-esteem and a fear that things won't work out. She has a hot/cold bond with ex-husband Baxter, father to Roscoe. Violet's father used to beat her up, so there's no contact. Christy is emotionally wounded, and her need to prove herself as a mother tends to get in the way of her ability to relate to men. Bonnie loves sex for sex's sake and is sexually confident, unlike her daughter. The love of her life is Christy's dad Alvin, who Bonnie dates again while living with Christy. Unfortunately, Alvin dies while they are having sex. Marjorie has affairs on the side.

GENDER-BENDING WITH ROLE-CHOICES CASE STUDIES: *The Tunnel* and *Elementary*

The Tunnel and *Elementary*, both crime series with male and female "cop" partnerships, are great examples of both main characters switching up conventionally "masculine" and "feminine" Role-Choices. The UK/France–based *The Tunnel* is heavily serialized, while New York–based *Elementary* is episodic with serialized elements.

The Tunnel: Karl: Middle aged, married, father, shabby, cynical. Nurturing, emotionally empathetic, intuitive (caring Mother Role-Choice). Emotionally wounded (grieving Victim). Unfaithful (guilty Lover).
Elise: Young, glamorous, French, single, no kids. On the autistic spectrum, rational, objective, gets results through logical deduction (cold Boss). Deeply buried emotional pain (partial Victim). Loves Sex (liberated Lover).

Elementary: Watson: Single, forties, glamorous, Asian, self-composed, calm. Ex-surgeon (wounded Healer, broken Caryatid). Father issues (damaged Child). Committed to partnership (Sorority/Fraternity). Trying to solve quests (Hero). Knowing who she is but not quite there (Incomplete Heroine).
Sherlock: Single, forties, English eccentric, genius. Drug addict (Victim). Father issues (damaged Child). Committed to partnerships

(Sorority/Fraternity). Defiant sleuth (Rebel/Hero). Trying to find self and place in the world (Outsider and Incomplete Heroine).

Creating Series Themes

Not only does a great television series need a unique and memorable female character, or cast of characters in an ensemble, it demands a distinguishing and underpinning theme that the protagonist's journey will illuminate. Once you have found it, this theme will shape all the characters' arcs across episodes and seasons. It will be like a guiding principle.

Themes reflect the writer's worldview on a very deep level; they are part of your motivation behind the choice of character and the journey she goes on. Themes at their most basic present the underlying message behind your story. It's the secret message you want to whisper in the ears of your audience so that when they leave the living room, they think about and perhaps feel validated by the deeper questions your series is exploring. One of your theme's main jobs is audience satisfaction. This doesn't mean it is a deep and worthy theme; it could be something fairly simple, like "a true friend goes the distance, whatever life throws up," but it will be buried underneath all the action, twists, and turns in your character's life.

You cannot rush finding your theme. Like cream, themes rise to the top with every story document you produce in the early stages of developing your idea. If you try and find your theme too early, you can put yourself under unnecessary pressure to shoehorn characters and plots into a theme that might not be quite right. You will have a reciprocal relationship with your theme: the theme will reveal something about you, but you will want to reveal something about it! Your story and its theme are always going to be deeply influenced by your own philosophies about life, which are drawn from your own life experiences.

Your job is to simultaneously work on your characters and your story in their early stages of development. Whatever your process, it takes some work to find your theme. Even if you have one at the beginning, be open to change. If don't have one, but have a vague idea, like *love and hate in an artists' community*, then do the development work and the real theme will come. When it does, it will be more specific, and have a slant. Like *"art can be destroyed by those who treasure it most."* It should feel like Robert McKee's Controlling Idea in *Story*, which is a very good guide to theme. Your theme is a golden and priceless product of an alchemical process involving your unconscious, your creativity, and your storytelling talent. It probably reflects what you stand for as a person. Remember, themes work best when they are subliminal. Your audience will be so caught up with your character, her fascinating M-Factor, her problems, and her world that they won't be actively looking for it anyway. All the same, it has to be there, working its magic.

The Metaphoric Wound

This is a model that you might find useful in developing the deeper theme of your series. It's also a model that can assist with character development, which is never a bad thing! Like all the creative exercises and strategies in this book, the Metaphoric Wound isn't a "rule" or a "dramaturgical truth," but offers an aid to your creative story-building process. Its main aim is to connect your main characters to the wider theme of your series. While it is equally applicable to writing film, it's useful for television because it may shed light on the longer, more meandering, unfolding emotional journey of your female characters across episodes, seasons, and series.

All protagonists, like all humans, carry around unresolved wounds to some degree or other. These form the scar tissues incurred by earlier life that may or may not be visible to the audience. If she is lucky, your protagonist will heal this pain over the course of her story. This is what happens in most transformational journeys in feature films with "up" endings. If she isn't so lucky, the story will explore her pain rather than resolve it. This could result in the story having an ambiguous ending, thematically. It is possible that your story actually is all about the worst thing to happen to your character so far in her life. It's about her getting the scar tissue!

In TV, sometimes this dreadful occurrence will be in the pilot, or in a carefully positioned flashback. It is revealed because it lets the audience into the protagonist's private and internal world a little more deeply. As we all have wounds ourselves, we instantly feel more empathy with the main characters. Sometimes it isn't spelt out, it is alluded to. But we get a sense that bad stuff's gone down, and this intrigues us.

Your protagonist will heal her wounds, or be left damaged to some extent. Your story might end up saying there is no chance for healing, offering a bleak ending.

The healing of your protagonist's pain is directly linked to the theme via the Metaphoric Wound. So it can be helpful to work out what this could be. The Metaphoric Wound is symbolic of your protagonist's unresolved deeper pain. That private and internal pain reverberates out, like an echo resounding around the valley of your narrative. The theme — your deepest idea and message — echoes it. The supporting characters reflect it. The Metaphoric Wound is possibly the deepest layer of meaning in your story, even deeper than the theme. In this way, once you find out what your Metaphoric Wound is, it can help you find your theme.

***The Metaphoric Wound is the deepest pain
experienced by your character. It is also visible
metaphorically in the wider world of her story.***

The Metaphoric Wound can be seen in the following levels of
your story world:

The Wider Culture: The Metaphoric Wound can be seen in
the values and customs of the wider world; it will impact
the community.

The Community: The Metaphoric Wound can function in the way
your character's community is organized, and how people within
the community treat each other. In turn it can affect the family.

The Family: The Metaphoric Wound is often generated here,
and it can be seen in how the family functions as a group. Your
character can be wounded by her experiences here.

The Individual: A Metaphoric Wound caused by the family or a
family member will have a particular effect on your character
and will represent her deepest pain.

Remember, the more you work on your character's
internal conflicts, the more easily you will be able to find
the Metaphoric Wound. Working on internal conflicts can be
demanding, because it takes you as writer to the nebulous and
darker recesses of your character's mind. It's hard work and
difficult for you to go there as a writer because you will to some
extent be drawing on your own internal conflicts. If you can
think about your own Internal Wounds and Gifts, you might be
able to see the Metaphoric Wound in your own life. We all have
them, and we usually get a sense of them when we come up
against the same patterns in life and relationships. If you don't
heal them, they might be reflected in the stories you choose
to tell (if you subscribe to the notion that we are constantly
working out issues through creative expression).

Finding the Metaphoric Wound

To find the Metaphoric Wound, first do the Gifts and Wounds exercise below to help you brainstorm some of the deeper issues in your protagonist(s). You might wish to go back to the chapter on conflict and explore her internal struggles.

Gifts And Wounds
⌁ QUESTIONNAIRE ⌁

1. What is the worst thing that has ever happened to you?
2. How does it make you feel now?
3. How do you cope with it?
4. Are there any people in your life who make you feel bad about yourself? Why?
5. How do you behave when you are around people who make you feel bad about yourself?
6. How would you like to change your behavior toward them?
7. How do you make yourself feel good?
8. Who makes you feel good about yourself?
9. What kind of relationship would you like to develop with people who make you feel good?
10. If you could make a wish, what would it be?

Now look at some of the answers. Try to boil down the "worst things" that ever happened to a few core issues. Next, you are going to delve into your character's backstory, and then you have to look at the "here and now" of her world in the story. The things you are looking for are her Internal Wound, her Internal Gift, her External Gift, and her External Wound. These are defined below.

Internal Wound: This is the most deeply felt emotional pain that your heroine has ever experienced. For a lot of people, this is caused in childhood by a parental figure or a severely traumatic event. You have to work out what this is for your character by looking deeply into her past and present. It may be buried and deeply repressed, but comes out in how she is functioning in relation to herself and other people. And, of course, your story might reveal what caused her Internal Wound, and how she lives and deals with it.

Take the core-deep pains that you have selected and try to reduce them to a single one. For example, maternal/paternal abuse, maternal/paternal abandonment, parental neglect, loss of a sibling, or sexual abuse.

Internal Gift: Your character's Internal Gift is her best coping mechanism, one she has developed to protect herself from a deep Internal Wound. You can see it as a defense mechanism in psychological terms. It doesn't have to be very positive. A self-harmer might find the experience of cutting herself a release. She might be abrasive to anyone new she meets. She might self-sabotage at every opportunity. This is her coping mechanism, her Internal Gift. You might think "Gift" is not really the right word for a potentially troublesome way of behaving that doesn't lead to fulfillment, but it quite effectively reflects the high value your character places on this defense mechanism.

Try to pinpoint your character's coping mechanism, a trait or way of being that somehow shields her and helps her deal with the unresolved pain caused by her Internal Wound.

External Gift: An External Gift is our symbolic happily-ever-after. It's the happiest and most content we could be if certain things fell into place in our lives. For your character, see it as a potential life, which is there for the taking if only she could somehow get there and be able to accept it. It might seem like a longshot, depending on how damaged she is and how dark her world is. The External Gift can be a lifestyle, a relationship, or a way of being functional. But if she could accept the External Gift, emotionally, and be open to it, she would get a lot of happiness from it. The External Gift is so powerful, it could solve all your character's problems. It is like the invisible fairy godmother working her magic, using a wound to make the scar tissue go away.

Now move away from the backstory and into the here and now of your character's world. Ask yourself what in her story is potentially the best thing that could happen to her, and is a real possibility. Who or what in the story symbolizes the potential for the most happiness? Who or what could help her be healed, be all she has the potential to be? Clue: For a television character in a long-running series, this gift has to be very far away indeed.

External Wound: The External Wound is the biggest source of outside conflict that affects your character as it drags her into making choices under pressure that put her in peril — or those she loves in peril. It will consume most of her day-to-day being and thinking and be the focus of her external world. It is the aspect of her life that she has to deal and cope with because it is there, in her face, being a massive issue! This is her External Wound.

Don't worry if you aren't sure. Brainstorm these, and try to narrow them down to what feels the most absolute for each.

Staying in the story, ask yourself what your character's biggest problem is. You might want to look at this as the biggest external obstacle she has to solve in the story, sometimes presented by the antagonist, or sometimes by the quest that she has chosen.

The following Metaphoric Wound Principles are important to understand if you want to see how your character's experience reverberates around your story world.

1. Your character's Internal Gift, her coping mechanism, feeds the External Wound. Because she has the defense mechanism, it keeps her stuck.

2. The Internal Gift is a paradox. It helps her cope, but it gets in the way of her solving her actual problem.

3. The External Wound feeds the unresolved Internal Wound. In other words, your character's failure to resolve her inner problem means that she is somehow, consciously or unconsciously, contributing to her own difficulties.

4. The Internal Gift has to be given up or sacrificed to achieve the External Gift.

5. Healing the Internal Wound achieves the External Gift.

6. On a thematic level, the Metaphoric Wound of your story is your Heroine's Internal Wound.

7. The Metaphoric Wound may or may not be healed in the story. What happens to the protagonist by the end of her journey will leave either an open Metaphoric Wound, a healed Metaphoric Wound, or a really rotten and poisoned Metaphoric Wound.

You can see that the Metaphoric Wound, stemming from the character's deepest inner conflicts, is reflected in all levels of the story's world. Finding it may help you determine the themes and ideas that concern your story, here woven into the fabric of your character.

Remember that the Metaphoric Wound is only one way of finding your theme. We all have our own processes. You might be a writer for whom a certain theme — the message you really want to get across — is your very first motivating factor to write the story.

Metaphoric Wound Case Study:
Orange Is the New Black

Main Character: Piper Chapman is a young, middle-class woman who is sentenced to eighteen months in prison. She was named part of a drug-smuggling ring in the case of her ex-lesbian lover, Alex Vause. Piper is a WASP, blonde, beautiful, and seemingly privileged, so it is shocking that she is going to face the unthinkable and be banged up with lowlifes and "real" criminals. The series starts with Piper coming to terms with her imminent incarceration, and dealing with it with her supportive fiancé Larry. She enters jail like a lamb to the slaughter, knowing nothing about the inmate culture and with everything to learn if she is to survive. At the time of writing, Season 3 shows a very different Piper, now a toughened inmate, badass and running her own dirty-panties smuggling operation with the help of a corrupt prison officer.

Piper: Internal Wound: Neglectful Parents (liars, keeping up appearances)
Internal Gift: Narcissistic merging, lack of boundaries
External Wound: Prison, encouraging criminality
External Gift: Freedom with self-awareness and self-discipline

Piper's Internal Gift feeds her External Wound: her lack of boundaries resulted in her being a drug mule for her girlfriend Vause, leading to incarceration. The relationship itself is somewhat compulsive for both, driven by desire and game-playing rather than honesty and trust. But it's electric for both; each is addicted to the other. However, if Piper is ever going to shed "risk" from her life, she will have to give up her Internal Gift. To be mature, she needs to learn to accept boundaries in life and relationships. Everything originates from her Internal Wound, having parents who did not instill a sense of truth. Her father was unfaithful and stayed married to keep up appearances, and her mother did not want to face this truth and denied the affair, even to Piper, who witnessed it.

Piper's unresolved Internal Wound, parental neglect manifested through immorality and lies, contributes to the External Wound of prison. The funny thing is, while Piper consciously knows lies are part of her family culture, she accepts that she is a product of them rather than do anything about the situation. As prison is also run by "liars," officers who are regularly criminal themselves, prison isn't exactly the correctional environment it could be. By continuing her illegal schemes inside, Piper risks getting caught and having her sentence extended. Her life is a hell of her own making. She is also lying to herself about who she really is, playing a role and convincing herself she's okay with being a merciless boss. She isn't. It is actually destroying her.

The show over three seasons has evolved into an ensemble prison drama in which Piper is now one of several memorable inmates. There isn't space to find all the characters' Internal and External Wounds and Gifts, but here are some favorites:

Vause: Internal Wound: Parental Neglect (absent father, inadequate mother)
Internal Gift: Self-serving strategist
External Wound: Imprisonment with fear of death from drug-cartel boss
External Gift: Happy, safe freedom, and loved by Piper

Red: Internal Wound: Parental Neglect
Internal Gift: Control freak
External Wound: Staying in charge of her prison family
External Gift: Freedom, her own business

Taystee: Internal Wound: Parental abandonment
Internal Gift: Getting overly attached, neediness

External Wound: No family outside prison

External Gift: Freedom with good job and loving family

Pennsatucky: Internal Wound: Parental neglect (absent father, abusive mother)

Internal Gift: Self-destruction and addiction

External Wound: Imprisonment and no self-esteem

External Gift: Freedom with self-respect, self-confidence, and a respectful relationship

Nichols: Internal Wound: Maternal neglect (cold mother)

Internal Gift: Heroin addiction

External Wound: Supermax

External Gift: Freedom, addiction free, and in loving relationship with a woman

Boo: Internal Wound: Maternal neglect

Internal Gift: Defiant and tough loner

External Wound: Imprisonment, family disapproval

External Gift: Freedom, functional lesbian relationship, acceptance by family

Crazy Eyes: Internal Wound: Parental abandonment and neglect

Internal Gift: Paranoid fantasist

External Wound: Nobody loving or understanding her

External Gift: Being loved, understood, and accepted

The shared Internal Wound of all the characters in *Orange Is the New Black* is a tough start in life, all being victims of abuse, abandonment, or neglect in one form or another (and normally at the hands of parental figures). The Metaphoric Wound is Abusive Care, a symbolic form of the parental mistreatment found in an unequal society that encourages criminality in the neglected and disadvantaged. Can the series's Metaphoric Wound be healed? This is where there is monumental dramatic irony; prison is actually corrupt as a system, run by cynics, misogynists, racists, faceless corporate profiteers, drug smugglers, and rapists.

The series themes seem to suggest that society is no better, and is not going to change. Society does not care for the disadvantaged; only individuals can do that for each other. The inmates have no chance or need to change when criminally minded staff have the power. To fight back, the inmates have their own culture of female gangs, with the protection of the Mom of their gang (and its other members). The women look out for their own, conditional on everyone staying in line and honoring the rules of the gang. Nurturing and not-so-nurturing relationships do spring up, and healing of the Internal Wounds does take place; the problem is, these happen within the prison bubble. By supporting each other, some of the inmates are able to relinquish their Internal Gifts:

* Pennsatucky develops more self-esteem through the support of Boo, so is able to respect herself more.

* Crazy Eyes discovers her creative gifts, helping her low self-esteem issues.

* Vause walks away from Piper's schemes, avoiding big trouble.

* Boo becomes more caring of another person by looking out for Pennsatucky.

* Taystee becomes the Mom of her gang. Where she was once a needy girl, she's now reclaiming her power.

This "letting go" of Internal Gifts might not be sustainable outside prison walls. For example, Taystee is excited about being released, but when she gets out and can't locate her "adopted" gangbanger mom Vee, she falls apart and ends up inside again within weeks for breaking the terms of her parole. She later admits she didn't like it outside anyway and missed her best friend. Nichols is a tragic case, a charismatic, life-loving character who's deeply wounded on the inside. In life outside, she used drugs as escapism and to obtain a false feeling of comfort. She is someone so driven by her addiction, she can't let this Internal Gift go and rid herself of the desire for drugs. Hiding some heroin she discovers results in her lockup in the maximum-security prison down the road. In short, all the relinquishing of the Internal Gifts is happening inside prison, which is also the External Wound — the biggest problem — for most of the women.

The Metaphoric Wound in *Orange Is the New Black* is found in all layers of the world:

Individually: every inmate has been neglected and abused. The Warden and COs also have wounds from childhood.

Family: The prison Moms offer tough love. Fall foul, and the "daughter" can be rejected. She is punished and has to earn her way back into the prison family the hard way. The other gang members will shun her. When Piper insults Red's food, she is left to starve, and served tampons in her breakfast.

Community: The wider inmate community is tough-going. Without power or protection, you are lonely and vulnerable. Women find solidarity and tenderness through their gangs, their one-on-one relationships, and ad hoc interactions. Female solidarity is not guaranteed.

Staff: The prison, as a community, is punitive rather than correctional. Inhumane degradation is frequent. Unjust measures and corruption rule the day; the inmates are frequently the target of the anger, misogyny, and unresolved issues of the staff.

Outside: Flashbacks reveal a tough society for most of the inmates, particularly the Mexican and black inmates who suffer from racism and lack of opportunity. The flashbacks frequently show how the Internal Wound was initially caused, or show an incident where the Internal Wound is being prodded.

In *Orange Is the New Black*, the theme could be one of the following:

Prison might give you the family you never had, but you can't take it with you

or

Prison isn't correctional, inmate solidarity is

or

In a corrupt society, going straight is hard to do.

Examples of the Metaphoric Wound in TV series:
Penny Dreadful: The Metaphoric Wound is Guilty Failure about one's dark side. Every character feels guilty about what or who they have lost due to their own lack of morality or inherent badness.
Elementary: The Metaphoric Wound is Parental Abandonment. Sherlock's mother died, and his father is a monster to him. This leads to his addiction, in which he abandons responsibility for himself and others. Joan lost her father, who was mentally ill and abandoned the family. Her desire to achieve as a surgeon also led to failure, forcing her to abandon her profession.

⌒ *EXERCISE* ⌒
Getting to Know Metaphoric Wounds

If you are developing a series, try to work out the Metaphoric Wound and see if this helps you refine your theme.

Alternatively, watch your favorite show and see if you can work out the Metaphoric Wound and the theme.

CHAPTER 9

The Unsung Female Protagonist in Uncharted Territory

*B*y now you are well on the way to knowing who your female protagonist is, the story she's leading, and all the factors that will make her compelling, unique, and completely unforgettable. If you haven't got a project on the go, maybe your imagination has been fired up by some of the ideas.

Wouldn't it be great if your next heroine is one of those truly unforgettable female characters who is remembered for decades? Clever writers can dream up characters that somehow represent exactly what the audience needs to see and hear, that sum up the zeitgeist, and that ring true.

There are still some grossly underrepresented female character archetypes in film and TV. Lesbians, trans women to men, disabled women, women of different ethnic groups, women with disabilities. The factor unifying all women's lives is aging. In most cultures, this sees women beginning to feel invisible, certainly in terms of attractiveness — and to some extent, in terms of being out in the world on one's own. There is huge scope for diverse older female protagonists across all genres.

The good news is that empowering and diverse female protagonists continue to flourish on screen, and even more so in the imagination of writers. And as diversity is embraced by the industry, they are increasing year by year. A book like this will hopefully not be needed as gender and diversity awareness continues to thrive.

Remember that the kinds of produced films and shows that you like to watch might not be the ones you are best at writing. Our needs for entertainment aren't necessarily compatible with our creative skillsets. Try to find a character, a genre, and themes that give you a great sense of creative momentum as you sit down to write.

- What kind of films or TV shows with a woman in the lead would you like to see?
- What have you never seen a female character do or be?
- What stories are yet to be told?
- What changes do you anticipate in women's lives over the next decade?
- What formats and genres do you feel most comfortable writing for? Are these the same as the ones you like watching?

It is very common to discover that the female character (or any character for that matter) or idea you have is scarily similar to one you discover in a produced show or film. It may be that you are in a writers' group or writing class and someone is writing something similar to your project or story terrain. It is most unlikely that the character or story is exactly the same as yours. Each writer is unique, and each writer's voice and style are unique.

The good news is that this reflects your attunement with the zeitgeist and current ideas. The bad news is you may have to dramatically alter aspects of your story or premise to keep the momentum (and your own enthusiasm for your character) going. With the rapid development of many new female characters on screen, arguably the risks of creative overlap may increase. For instance, in the time since the first edition of this book was published, there has been a rise in films and shows that explore female solidarity, the complex reality of female friendship, the mother/daughter relationship, and darker, conflicted heroines. *Brave, Black Swan, Bridesmaids, Orange Is the New Black, Conviction*, and *Girls* have all pushed the boundaries of female-driven stories. Ensemble shows like *Justified, Penny Dreadful*, and *The Walking Dead* have female characters that are no longer sidekicks or less complicated or conflicted than the male characters. Female protagonists are becoming increasingly violent, immoral, and twisted.

The terrain for female characters is wide open and there are still plenty of undiscovered places for them — and you as writers — to roam.

Transmedia Female Protagonists

In the digitally converged world, writers need to be skilled in developing story worlds and generating stories across many platforms. If you write a screenplay or a novel, it may become a film. There may be a spinoff TV series, a game, an app, a range of merchandise. As far as novice writers are concerned, your first story, whether it's a screenplay, novel, short story, or another format, will probably be the one closest to your heart. So what does this mean for your female protagonist? What does "transmedia storytelling" mean as far as gender representation goes?

Developing stories with a cast of characters across platforms is a great way of working out if you have an unconscious attitude about the kinds of stories you give male and female characters, and whether your use of conflict, union, POV, themes, tone, and other elements change. A different format might mean a different character leads the story, perhaps someone who was secondary in another format, such as the novel.

In terms of gender representation across platforms, some of the following changes might occur:

* Your protagonist might be older or younger, depending on whether the format is taking place in a different time.

* She might look different. How has her appearance changed?

* She might feel very differently about her life. What does she feel? What does she want? What values and attitudes does your older protagonist possess? How do these change in comparison with her older or younger self?

* How have opportunities for women changed across timescales? If all the narratives are in the same time period, how can you define the social, economic, cultural, and political issues affecting women?

* What is her dramatic function? Is she the protagonist, secondary character, or tertiary character, or has she become an absent (or even dead) character? If absent, does she have an impact on the remaining characters?

* If she isn't the protagonist, how does she relate to the protagonist?

* What SuperTheme influences the new story? Is it the same as the SuperTheme of the original story?

Norma Bates in *Bates Motel*

In Alfred Hitchcock's *Psycho*, Norma Bates, we would all agree, isn't in good shape. She's a mummified corpse in a cellar of the home owned by Norman Bates. In his mind, Norma is very much alive. He even believes she is mentally ill. Norman enters a psychotic state where he becomes Norma, and dresses up in her clothes. He murders girls who are sexually alluring to him. As Norma, Norman believes these girls are sluts, and she is jealous of their appeal to Norman, and his vulnerability to them. Much later we find out that Norma and her lover died in a murder-suicide ten years earlier. After Norman murders a young woman, he is finally found out and locked away.

For most of the TV series *Bates Motel*, Norma is very much alive. She's the overprotective mother of the very troubled teenager Norman. The TV series enables Norma to go from mummification to momification, and in doing so become one of the most fascinating female characters on TV. The writers have brilliantly and imaginatively plundered the original story to create a very contemporary world for the series.

The pathologically entwined relationship of Norma and Norman brings to life and gives an entirely new spin on what was essentially *Psycho*'s backstory. The writers are able to select key moments, images, objects, and character actions from the original film and weave them creatively into the contemporary version. Even the house and motel rooms are brought to life in *Bates Motel* as locations where key events take place and that resonate with the atrocities of *Psycho*. These include Norman's taxidermy, hiding the dirty dressing gown resulting from one of his murders, and hiding a body in one of the motel rooms.

After the death of her husband, Norman's father, Norma sets up a new life in White Pine Bay, Oregon, to run the Bates

Motel. As a character, Norma is incredibly complex: girly, vulnerable, seductive, manipulative, impulsive, outspoken, frightened, courageous, eccentric, no-nonsense. She has a vintage look to her, is glamorous and blonde, and drives an older model Mercedes. Norma is pathologically obsessed with Norman, unable to admit to herself how mentally ill he is. She encourages the unhealthy bond between her and Norman, ridden by guilt if he is upset, and overcompensates, cooking him his favorite food and curling up on the sofa together. She encourages him to feel like the man of the house, and panders to his need to protect her. Often they lie in bed together, unhealthily close. Norma encourages his obsessive feelings about her, as they make her feel safe and wanted. They share a love of vintage movies, and both don't easily fit in the world, feeling safest when together. Her feelings toward her other, older son Dylan, born from an incestuous relationship she had with her own brother, slowly grow from repulsion to fondness.

With no chance of an Oedipus complex, Norman gets increasingly powerful. His psychopathic tendencies slowly but surely take over. Knowing Norman murders, Norma cannot admit it to herself. She goes to great lengths to pretend Norman's blackouts are manageable if she protects him. Norma is incredibly good at getting men to look after her. This includes the local Sheriff Romero, who marries Norma so she can get medical help for Norman when he starts going off the rails. With Norman institutionalized, Norma finally has a chance at happiness. Her vulnerability to Norman's manipulative powers over her remains intact, however. To keep his mother to himself, Norman embarks on a murder/suicide bid, but only manages to kill Norma. Unable to let her go even in death, he digs her body up and takes it home. Norma comes back to life in the form of Norman's delusional image, happily playing the piano at Christmas.

An interesting Metaphoric Wound lies at the heart of *Bates Motel*, that of the Incestuous Parent, on a symbolic level. In *Psycho*, the Metaphoric Wound could be said to be the *Abandoning Parent*; a pathologically jealous Norman murders both his mother and her boyfriend in a fit of jealousy, and stages it as a murder-suicide. In *Bates Motel*, Norma relates to this through the inner conflict roiled from her experiences as an abused child, resulting in an inability to form proper boundaries. She had a sexual relationship with her brother Caleb for many years, and her relationship with Norman is emotionally incestuous. Norman is also an abuse survivor who witnessed Norma's violence and rape by his father at a very young age. He even held Norma's hand, hiding under her bed while she was being raped. This deeply repressed internal conflict forms part of his need to identify as Norma; in his fantasy, she is always sassy, in control, smart-talking, and invincible.

Dylan, the son of Caleb and Norma, as a child of incest who has been rejected by both parents, suffers the Internal Wound of not being good enough. While he heals some of the rift with Norma, he knows he will never come close to receiving the love that Norman gets. The separation of both parents enables Dylan to form his own values about what constitutes a good relationship, and to find love outside the family, which he manages with the loving Emma. Sheriff Romero, who marries Norma to help her institutionalize Norman by means of his health-insurance policy, deeply loves her. He transgresses his professional boundaries to help her time and time again, reflecting the symbolically incestuous wound. The wider community is ruled by wealthy marijuana drug lords who wield considerable power and influence. This reflects a dark, unboundaried underbelly that resonates with the Metaphoric Wound.

The opportunities for women in Norma's life in *Bates Motel* are very different than those available in *Psycho*. In many respects Norma is an independent single mother who multitasks to financially provide for her son while she emotionally parents him and acts as a "mother." The town has many independent women — drug dealers, bank workers, and police officers — depicting a real change in women's opportunities from the 1960s version. Norman calls Norma "Mother" rather than "Mom" or "Norma" as Dylan does. Not only does this reinforce his old-fashioned attitude, it reminds us of the Mother character that controls Norman's mind in *Psycho*.

Norma and Norman's shared love of the retro and the vintage, in music, films, and clothes, forms a clever play on the inversion of time periods. As Norman gets increasingly ill, becoming "Mother" in his blackouts, he starts wearing Norma's clothes such as her dressing gown. Norman's mental disorder in *Bates Motel* has its fair share of interventions such as therapy and residential care; those who know him recognize he has issues. As a high-functioning manipulative psychopath, we are convinced that Norman can wriggle out of the professional help he receives, and continue to manipulate his mother; as a woman wracked by maternal guilt, we can see Norma will have no chance against him.

Composite Heroines

All our characters emerge from very complex processes and inspirations. The exercises and models in the book have hopefully given you some ways of getting started or working on a character you already have in mind or in development. The final exercise, "Composite, Contrary, and Contentious Female Character," is a way of thinking about your character in terms of your own creative journey and how she takes her place amongst all of your projects. A Composite Female Character is a symbolic female character that reflects you as a writer and inventor. She stands for your deepest themes and concerns, your original voice, and the forms of support and inspiration you have encountered in your journey as a writer.

Composite, Contrary, and Contentious Female Character Exercise

It's best to do this exercise as a brainstorm. You can divide a sheet of paper into two halves and answer the questions to 1 and 2 in the different columns.

1. Ask yourself:
   * Which women in your own life have inspired you?
   * Who would you say is the most amazing woman in your life? Why?
   * What qualities do you like and admire in females?
   * What qualities/traits do you not like or admire in females?
   * Which female do you like to have fun with? Why?
   * Which female do you turn to for emotional support? Why?
   * Which female has hurt you the most? Why?
   * What annoys and irritates you about women?
   * Who is your favorite true-life female hero? This can be somebody you know or don't know.
   * Who are your favorite female actors? Why? What roles have they played that you particularly liked?
   * How would you describe your own attitude toward feminism?

2. Now, turn to look at all your female characters across different projects. Your task is to consider the following questions and try to identify any commonalities. Ask yourself:

- What genres do you tend to write in? Why?
- What SuperThemes do they identify with?
- What Role-Choices do they explore?
- Which gender do your characters instinctively trust?
- What internal conflicts do they suffer?
- Who are their biggest antagonists?
- Is there female solidarity in their worlds? How?
- Do your characters relate to your own feminist views?
- What are their ages/ethnicities/abilities?
- What M-factors?
- What kinds of themes do they represent?

When you've finished, use a color highlighter to identify shared traits, ideas, or other links (common themes) between the two lists of answers. With another color highlighter, mark words that stand out or that seem unconnected.

3. Your task now is to create a character that represents all the common themes in your life and work. This is your **Composite Female Character**. She represents the core ideas that you like to explore when writing a female character.

4. Now, create a character out of the standout, unconnected themes. This is your **Contrary Female Character**. She represents a character who is truly unique. If developed, she has the potential to push your themes in a new direction.

5. Finally, take another look at the list of common themes and ideas. Make a note of their *opposite values*. Now try to create a character type using these opposite values. This is your **Contentious Female Character**. She represents the female characters you tend to *avoid* creating. If developed, she has the potential to completely revolutionize your storytelling. She may take you into uncharted narrative territory!

If you are so inspired, give your favorite of these three characters a name and a story. Then choose the right genre for the project. Perhaps it will become your next one.

CHAPTER 10

Bringing It All Together: An Analysis of Katniss Everdeen in The Hunger Games Films

K atniss Everdeen is the young female protagonist of the *Hunger Games* films: *The Hunger Games*, *The Hunger Games: Catching Fire*, *The Hunger Games: Mockingjay — Part 1*, and *The Hunger Games: Mockingjay — Part 2*, adapted from the successful novels by Suzanne Collins. Katniss symbolizes a strong and memorable female character with a complex emotional arc as she develops into a rebel fighter.

Set in the futuristic dystopia of Panem, the story follows Katniss as she takes part in the brutal reality TV show called *The Hunger Games* in which "Tributes" compete against each other in a fight to the death. The last survivor is crowned Victor. The fighting occurs in a different arena each year, a remote place that is controlled virtually by a team of computer technologists overseen by the Gamemaker. The Hunger Games are a twisted way of ensuring social control by the brutal patriarchy based in the Capitol, lorded over by despot patriarch Snow. Panem comprises the Capitol and the thirteen Districts where the oppressed workers live grouped by trade. To pay penance for previous insurrection and an attempted but unsuccessful rebellion many years ago, the oppressed Districts have to offer up one boy and one girl to Panem as Tributes to fight in the annual Hunger Games. Over the four films Katniss Everdeen grows from being a volunteer Tribute to a leader of the rebellion. Her emotional journey is complex, contradictory, and emotionally compelling. While it is a journey to leadership, it is equally a journey to finding identity.

SuperTheme

The dominant SuperTheme of the Hunger Games is Fighting Femininity. Katniss identifies as a freedom fighter, first on a very personal level, to save her sister's life, and later on a much wider scale, as she decides to do all she can to support the rebellion. A negative masculine patriarchal regime is characterized by its extreme violence against victims, starvation of oppressed people, and corrupt ruling elite in the Capitol who are vain, fashion-obsessed, greedy, and wasteful of resources. Extreme poverty and excessive wealth divide the people. Katniss believes in solidarity. She is motivated to support the weak and the helpless with a determination to do all she can to bring the regime down.

M-Factor

Katniss's most compulsive need is: To be **strong to help her family** and those she loves.

Her most irreverent trait is **defiance** in the face of abusive power.

Her most charismatic trait is **staying positive and determined even in the face of hell.**

Katniss's M-Factor is **determined rebelliousness.**

She is memorable as she maintains a strict moral code of loyalty to, and protection of, those she loves while maintaining a core of defiance.

Role-Choices

Hero: Katniss is by nature a capable and loyal Hero who will sacrifice herself for those she loves and wants to protect, such as Prim, Peeta, and Rue. As she evolves, her heroism extends to her District when it revolts, and then later as she becomes the symbolic leader of the rebellion. However, Katniss can be an ambivalent Hero when her personal allegiances are threatened. Coin is a female Hero and commander (Boss) of the rebellion. Her heroism is unflinching and driven by a "means justify the ends" approach that brings her into conflict with Katniss. Haymitch is a fallen Hero, something of a louche, who frequently puts himself on the line for Katniss when she is endangered in the Arena. Gale, Katniss's boyfriend, is a more straightforward Hero in ideals — but he is not a leader. Peeta displays heroism for Katniss in the Arena. He saves her when she is hallucinating and unable to protect herself. He will happily die for her if necessity demands it.

Heroine: Katniss is a Questing Hero, on a mission in each Hunger Games to win, and later to fight in the rebellion. She is also a Questing Heroine, yearning for the love and connection of those closest to her while finding a sense of identity as others try to control and define her. This mix of Heroism and Heroinism makes her a compelling Tribute and audience favorite. Bravery mixed with nurturing and a need for love is a potent combination. Katniss is also an "Outsider Heroine" — someone from a poor District. She even proves herself an Incomplete Heroine as her love for Peeta evolves. Saving and protecting Peeta is mixed with her need to be with him, her feelings increasingly consumed by caring for him. Katniss's heroism inspires others around her. She gives hope through her combination of ruthlessness, bravery, compassion, and loyalty.

Mother: As their actual mother had a breakdown after the loss of their father, Katniss pretty much raises her sister. She is mother and father, nurturer and provider. Later, in the Games, she shows nurturing to the dying Rue, singing and holding her. She adorns Rue's body with white flowers, tending to her like a grieving mother. The brutal society lacks identification with a positive Mother Role-Choice. There is no nurturing of the people; they are starving. Food is a privilege of the rich. The poor have to trade their children's lives for nourishment.

Lover: Katniss is a conflicted and ambivalent Lover, and she effectively loves two men: Peeta and Gale. She is loyal to both, and for a long time cannot choose one over the other. With Gale, her love is characterized by duty and loyalty; with Peeta, her feelings are more complex because they have been through hell together. The society doesn't reflect much romance. The elite are too narcissistic and the poor are suffering too much to "enjoy" the fun of romance. Relationships that go the distance are based on love and trust.

Child: Children and young people under eighteen are the tragic victims of a cruel world. They live in fear of being chosen as Tributes. They are Victims trapped by their own needs: the more food they request, the more likely their names will be chosen. The elite are like spoiled, nasty children who want to watch their games with excitement and carelessness. This infantile self-interest is symptomatic of a society where nurturing is not valued.

Victim: Katniss doesn't identify as a fearful or helpless Victim when she is in the Arena. Her need to survive and protect always kicks in, even at her most vulnerable. Her core defiance is like a bedrock on which all her other emotions are based. Peeta, as a male lover to Katniss, is a Victim who needs supervision and protection. He is also a "heroic" Victim, someone who will sacrifice himself for the common good. When he is tortured, he is a double Victim; not only does he need saving from Snow and the Capitol, he needs saving from his brainwashed, destructive self.

Healer: During the Games, Katniss attempts to heal Peeta and Rue when they are both critically injured. Healing in the Games is reciprocal — both Rue and Peeta help heal Katniss when she is suffering from wasp stings. Prim, inspired by Katniss, decides to train as a doctor. On a wider level, Katniss is a Healer to an entire community by acting as an inspiration to weaker people ground down by poverty and lack of power.

Sorority: There are no female groupings depicting female solidarity in *The Hunger Games*. There is a "feminine" Sorority made up of Cinna and Effie, who are responsible for Katniss's image and adornment. Katniss accepts their attention since they look out for her, but not because she actually buys into looking pretty and wearing nice clothes. Conventional adornment is fairly meaningless to Katniss, but she will look the part if it helps her survive in the Arena. Feminism in terms of female solidarity doesn't exist in this world. Discrimination comes in the form of repression of social classes.

Caryatid/Amazon: As the social order is oppressive and morally bankrupt, Katniss does not identify as someone who wants to uphold it. She is forced into playing a role in the Games. Katniss is Amazonian, motivated to liberate the oppressed and bring down the regime. However, she will play her part as a benign Caryatid in the new social order.

Boss: Corrupt patriarch Snow is motivated by greed and cruelty. Like snowfall, he blankets the Districts in coldness, leaving them to starve in a wilderness.

Rebel: Shooting an apple out of the hand of the Gamemaker while she is training is a symbolic moment of the Rebel in Katniss. It has echoes of Robin Hood. She brings down the Games and later triggers the rebellion itself when she shoots her bow at the force field. She does this in anger and defiance. Like all Rebels with a defiant cause, she is momentarily unconcerned about the consequences. Haymitch identifies as a weak Rebel who will gradually grow in strength. He is alcoholic and cynical, reluctantly doing the bidding of his masters, but rebelling through drink.

Warrior: Katniss's skills as a warrior are characterized by her hunting abilities. As a Warrior in the Games, she is fearless and strong. During the rebellion she is never weak, but she is conflicted if her efforts in the propaganda put Peter's life at risk.

Fraternity: The rebellion is a Fraternity of questing heroes and warriors. Led by Coin, there is a strict hierarchy and chain of command.

Rival: The Tributes are all Rivals in the Arena. Peeta and Gale are rivals for Katniss's heart. Coin is Rival to Katniss, threatened by both the young woman's popularity and her value system.

Father: Katniss identifies with the "fathering" side of parenting in that she steps in for her absent father as provider (in the conventional "masculine" sense) since her mother is initially too weak to take on this role herself. Identifying with the masculine means that Katniss has no problem bonding with good men such as Haymitch and Cinna. It also makes her a good match for the brutal patriarch Snow. In the first *Hunger Games*, the women in her lives — Effie and her mother — are weak.

Phases

Identity Phases:

Transition: Upon her momentous decision to volunteer for her sister as a Tribute, Katniss is whisked out of her District and takes a physical journey by train to a completely alien world. She has no idea who to be and how to behave, quickly learning that her way of reacting to the strange environment and the stranger people — the louche Haymitch and the frivolous Effie — is not going to help her. She has fragmented memories of Peeta, the baker's boy, who is now her partner Tribute, and she does not know if she can trust him. She is thrown off balance, without a support system, facing probable death.

Maternal Lessons: Katniss doesn't have particularly strong women role models; her own mother was unable to cope after the death of her husband. However, female solidarity exists between Katniss and younger girls like Prim and Rue: Katniss takes on a maternal role at key points in their survival. Katniss doesn't rely on women or trust them as easily as she does men, although she gradually forms a bond with Effie. Coin is a female commander who is driven and tough. The

Hunger Games world doesn't show a feminist sorority that provides female solidarity, but the oppressed people who share "feminine" values of affiliation, unity, and togetherness do band together. The commanders of the rebellion are all female.

Father Distance: Katniss's real father is missed badly by the family, particularly by Katniss. Her easier allegiance with male figures indicates an unconscious identification with positive masculinity. Cinna, Haymitch, Gale, and Peeta all nurture and support Katniss. However, the society is brutally patriarchal. The Hunger Games themselves reflect this punishing and cruel patriarchal system that divides, rules, and destroys. It is an oligarchy that does not nurture the masses, only the corrupt elite.

Adornment: Katniss is frequently "dressed up" as a Tribute, to look her part as an interesting competitor. Fire is the main element in her costumes, which symbolizes her passion, power, and transformation. But this is an act for a televised game. Closer to her personal identity is the Mockingjay, the image of the brooch she wears in the Arena to protect her. Becoming the Mockingjay is a tortuous path for Katniss.

Relating Phases:

Self-Regulation: Katniss needs to learn how to make friends so she can gain sponsors. Being her hostile self will not help her in the Arena. She needs to self-regulate to do this.

Desire for Union: Katniss and Peeta's relationship develops in a Quarter Quell of the Hunger Games. She already knows he has deeper feelings for her beneath the public act of being a couple in love that they have to maintain. But Katniss's own feelings develop, and she kisses him sincerely. It looks like part of the act, but she is acting on spontaneous desire.

Loving Too Much: Katniss is not going to cooperate with the resistance unless they help Peeta escape from the Capitol. She is almost obsessed by her feelings for him, so much so that it further estranges her from Gale. When she sees what Snow's "peacekeepers" have done to her District, she is motivated to do all she can to help them. But it is still on the condition that they help Peeta.

Retreat: At the end of the story, Katniss and Peeta retreat together to where it all started, District 12, which is now a desolate landscape. The rebellion was successful, but Katniss has to be scapegoated for assassinating Coin against orders when she was supposed to kill Snow. She and Peeta, left alone, are able to love one another in peace. In time, they create a family, and nature heals the landscape, which grows lush and fertile.

Momentum Phases:

Violation: Katniss belongs to a violated people, workers who are starved and bled dry by their Masters. Any insurrection results in brutal repression, including floggings and public executions. While her core strength prevents her from being a coward, the sheer brutality of the Hunger Games is an acute violation of Katniss and the other Tributes. Many are killed within the first few minutes. They die of exposure, dehydration, and the manipulations of the game planner, who can create real threats — firebombs, hunting dogs, poisonous wasps, poison fog, and tidal waves — to add "danger" to the games. The fact that this is both entertainment and an expression of social control is equally sickening to Katniss. After the Games, she continues to be violated in the form of nightmares of the trauma.

Crossroads: Katniss and Gale twice deliberate on fleeing through the forest to get away. Both times they decide against it. Life-and-death decisions become Katniss's norm in her bid to survive the Games. The choice between Gale and Peeta is a frequent Crossroads for Katniss. She is torn for a long time.

Eruption: When Katniss aims at the force field during the Quell, she has reached boiling point; she doesn't care if she lives or dies so long as she can inflict some damage. Katniss will erupt when people let her down, don't play fair, or endanger those she loves. As an active and proactive protagonist, she isn't someone who puts up with situations for long or to stay quiet.

Path to Potential: Every time Katniss decides to take a heroic action as the Mockingjay leader, she is strong and resolved. Her ability to strategize and negotiate reflects her core strengths; she is someone who knows her mind and who will do whatever is necessary to protect others. While her journey is conflicted, scary, and full of loss, Katniss does not veer from brave responsibility for long. When she finally kills Coin, she knows exactly what she is doing, and will do it for the good of the people.

Layers of Conflict

Internal: Katniss's internal conflicts are chiefly spurred by the guilt she feels when she cannot protect those she loves. She has moral dilemmas when she wants to protect Peeta at the expense of other lives. She is conflicted when she has to learn to be something she isn't — someone who puts on appearances to win sponsors and allies.

Significant Other: Her relationship with Gale is not easy; he is threatened by the strength of her feelings for Peeta that are televised throughout Panem. Katniss, an honest person, cannot convincingly deny her feelings. This estranges Katniss and Gale. Ultimately, she leaves Gale, partly due to his role in Prim's death.

Family: Katniss's conflict with her mother in the first *Hunger Games* film is caused by her mother's weakness. This requires Katniss to pick up the pieces since she's the parental figure. She loses respect for her mother, and is angry with her. She has a deep internal sense of loss for her father. When Peeta is brainwashed by torture, Katniss is devastated. It consumes and deeply saddens her.

Community: During the games in the Arena, the "community" consists of the Tributes, the game's runners, and the audience. To achieve her ends, Katniss needs to learn to attract sponsors. She needs to learn the "rules of the game" even though she despises its sick and evil nature. She will always hate the practice of divide and rule through brutality. She has clear rivals in the form of other Tributes who literally want to kill her.

Culture: Katniss despises the values of Snow and the Capitol. They instill defiance, rebellion, and bravery in her. She has no fear in going against these.

World: Panem is a corrupt world. It needs a revolution to be healed. Katniss, as the Mockingjay, is the symbol of the fight.

Layers of Union

Internal: Katniss can rely on her skills as a hunter and on her strong foundation of courage. This gives her a strong sense of internal conviction and faith in herself. She is decisive under pressure. While it is not a world that offers many chances for "inner peace," Katniss is guided by a strong moral compass.

Significant Other: The well-being of Peeta is fundamental to Katniss's own peace of mind. She gets comfort from knowing he is safe, from their shared understanding of the horror of the Arena. It bonds them on a very deep level. Katniss can rely on Gale for being loyal and steadfast to the cause, but her feelings run deeper for Peeta. Ultimately, they share the same values, and Katniss comes to accept that she is in love with him.

Family: Prim offers Katniss love and admiration. Katniss's bravery heals her weak family. Her mother becomes stronger, and Prim trains as a doctor.

Community: The people of the Districts have a defiant will; they just need a catalyst, somebody to believe in. Katniss eventually finds pride in becoming their Mockingjay, the face of the rebellion.

Culture: While the regime's values are sick, Katniss believes in a better world. This gives her hope and drive.

Metaphoric Wound

Internal Wound: Katniss's deep wound is the loss of her father and the emotional abandonment (temporarily) by her mother.
Internal Gift: Katniss's defense mechanism is self-sacrifice.
External Wound: Surviving the Hunger Games and protecting Peeta.
External Gift: Safety and health for those she loves, and being happy with Peeta.

The metaphoric wound of *The Hunger Games* is the failure of society to protect the vulnerable. The wound will only be healed by the rebellion crushing the evil regime.

Gender Mindfulness

This book has hopefully encouraged you to consider how your characters are a product of many factors and contexts regarding gender; it is your unique imagination that will process these using invention, inspiration, and subjective choices. Being gender-mindful includes giving yourself space for invention when creating your characters, as well having a more critical mindset as you look at your characters dispassionately (if you ever can!). The free-ranging, impulse-driven, subconscious, uncanny, law-breaking, inconsistent, random, intuitive, and perceptive imagination that always seems to come up with the best ideas — those eureka moments that are borne out of right-side/back-burner percolation — is a tool of the art, craft, and trade of writing. Inspiration is one of the most essential elements of writing, and certainly the process that makes writing so enjoyable. You may come up with a spectacular female character, but being "gender-mindful" will enable you to question aspects of her representation. Is she a positive role model? Does it matter to you and why? Why is she saying/doing/thinking being that? Do other characters treat her differently? Is she what you intended?

If the book's exercises, strategies, approaches, and paradigms inspire reflections, insights, and inventions that are true to your creative vision for your female protagonist, then it has served its purpose. The book still isn't claiming to be "the truth," the right way, the only way, or the most "rigorous" way to deal with gender issues; neither does it draw particularly on any specific feminist thinking other than my own life as a woman, writer, human being, teacher, and student. As such, it aims to be a gynocentric, feminist-friendly, and holistic resource. You may never be able to control how your female character is received or judged, but you can at least know you gave her your best shot to become everything you and your creative unconscious and conscious mind hoped she would be, from the light-bulb moment of a very early idea through the polished draft you show to the world.

Good luck!

References and Further Reading & Viewing

Books

Francke, L. *Script Girls: Women Screenwriters in Hollywood.* BFI, London, 1994

Glyn, E. *The Elinor Glyn System of Writing.* Author's Press, 1922

Hudson, K. *The Virgin's Promise.* Michael Wiese Productions, Studio City, 2010

Jacey, H. *The Woman in the Story: Writing Memorable Female Characters.* Michael Wiese Productions, Studio City, 2010

Leonard, L. *The Wounded Woman: Healing the Father-Daughter Relationship.* Shambhala, Boston & London, 1982

McKee, R. *Story: Structure, Substance, Style, and the Principles of Screenwriting.* Methuen, 1999

Murdock, M. *The Heroine's Journey: Woman's Quest for Wholeness.* Shambhala, Boston, 1990

Pinkola Estés, C. *Women Who Run With the Wolves: Contacting the Power of the Wild Woman.* Rider, London, 1998

Seger, L. *When Women Call the Shots: The Developing Power and Influence of Women in Television and Film.* Henry Holt, New York, 1996

Vogler, C. *The Writer's Journey: Mythic Structure for Storytellers and Screenwriters.* Pan, 1999

Television

Agent Carter (2015) Created by Christopher Markus, Stephen McFeely

Bates Motel (2013) Created by Anthony Cipriano, Carlton Cuse, Kerry Ehrin

The Blacklist (2013) Created by Jon Bokenkamp

Breaking Bad (2008) Created by Vince Gilligan

The Bridge (2013) Created by Hans Rosenfeldt

Broad City (2014) Created by Ilana Glazer, Abbi Jacobson

Call the Midwife (2012) Created by Heidi Thomas

The Catherine Tate Show (2004)

Conviction (2016) Created by Liz Friedlander, Liz Friedman

The Durrells (2016) Written by Simon Nye, based on *The Corfu Trilogy* by Gerald Durrell (2006)

Elementary (2012) Created by Robert Doherty

The Fall (2013) Created by Allan Cubitt

Game of Thrones (2011) Created by David Benioff, D.B. Weiss

Girls (2012) Created by Lena Dunham

Grace and Frankie (2015) Created by Marta Kauffman, Howard J. Morris

The Good Wife (2009) Created by Michelle King, Robert King

Hannibal (2013) Created by Bryan Fuller

Homeland (2011) Created by Alex Gansa, Howard Gordon

The Honourable Woman (2014) Written by Hugo Blick

House of Cards (2013) Created by Beau Willimon

How to Get Away With Murder (2014) Created by Peter Nowalk

Inside Amy Schumer (2013) Created by Daniel Powell, Amy Schumer

Jessica Jones (2015) Created by Melissa Rosenberg

Justified (2010) Created by Graham Yost

Love (2016) Created by Judd Apatow, Lesley Arfin, Paul Rust

Mad Men (2007) Created by Matthew Weiner

Madam Secretary (2014) Created by Barbara Hall

Mildred Pierce (2011) Adapted from *Mildred Pierce* by James M. Cain (1941)

Mom (2013) Created by Gemma Baker, Eddie Gorodetsky, Chuck Lorre

New Girl (2011) Created by Elizabeth Meriwether

Nurse Jackie (2009) Created by Liz Brixius, Evan Dunsky, Linda Wallem

Olive Kitteridge (2014) Based on the story by Elizabeth Strout (2008); Written by Jane Anderson

Orange Is the New Black (2013) Created by Jenji Kohan

Penny Dreadful (2014) Created by John Logan

The Real Housewives of Beverly Hills (2010) Created by Scott Dunlop

Scandal (2012) Created by Shonda Rhimes

Some Girls (2012) Created by Bernadette Davis

Supergirl (2015) Created by Ali Adler, Greg Berlanti, Andrew Kreisberg

Tracey Ullman's Show (2016)

Transparent (2014) Created by Jill Soloway

The Tunnel (2013) Adapted from *The Bridge* (2011)

Veep (2012) Created by Armando Iannucci

Veronica Mars (2004) Created by Rob Thomas

The Walking Dead (2010) Created by Frank Darabont

Film

Admission (2013) Written by Karen Croner, Jean Hanff Korelitz (book); Directed by Paul Weitz

The Age of Adaline (2015) Written by J. Mills Goodloe, Salvador Paskowitz; Directed by Lee Toland Krieger

Amelia (2009) Written by Ron Bass, Anna Hamilton Phelan, Susan Butler (book), Mary S. Lovell (book); Directed by Mira Nair

Avatar (2009) Written and Directed by James Cameron

The Aviator (2004) Written by John Logan; Directed by Martin Scorsese

The Babadook (2014) Written and Directed by Jennifer Kent

Becoming Jane (2007) Written by Kevin Hood, Sarah Williams, Jane Austen (letters); Directed by Julian Jarrold

Before Midnight (2013) Written by Richard Linklater, Julie Delpy, Ethan Hawke; Directed by Richard Linklater

Bessie (2015) Written by Dee Rees, Christopher Cleveland, Bettina Gilois; Directed by Dee Rees

The Best Exotic Marigold Hotel (2011) Written by Ol Parker, Deborah Moggach (book); Directed by John Madden

Big Eyes (2014) Written by Scott Alexander, Larry Karaszewski; Directed by Tim Burton

Black Swan (2010) Written by Mark Heyman, Andrés Heinz, John J. McLaughlin; Directed by Darren Aronofsky

Blue Jasmine (2013) Written and Directed by Woody Allen

Brave (2012) Written by Mark Andrews, Steve Purcell, Brenda Chapman, Irene Mecchi; Directed by Mark Andrews, Brenda Chapman, Steve Purcell

Bridesmaids (2011) Written by Kristen Wiig, Annie Mumolo; Directed by Paul Feig

Brooklyn (2015) Written by Nick Hornby, Colm Tóibín (book); Directed by John Crowley

Cake (2014) Written by Patrick Tobin; Directed by Daniel Barnz

Calendar Girls (2003) Written by Juliette Towhidi, Tim Firth; Directed by Nigel Cole

Carol (2015) Written by Phyllis Nagy, Patricia Highsmith (book); Directed by Todd Haynes

The Clouds of Sils Maria (2014) Written and Directed by Olivier Assayas

Coco Before Chanel (2009) Written by Anne Fontaine, Camille Fontaine, Edmonde Charles-Roux (book); Directed by Anne Fontaine

The Danish Girl (2015) Written by Lucinda Coxon, David Ebershoff (book); Directed by Tom Hooper

Dear White People (2014) Written and Directed by Justin Simien

The Dressmaker (2015) Written by P.J. Hogan, Jocelyn Moorhhouse, Rosalie Ham (book); Directed by Jocelyn Moorhouse

The DUFF (2015) Written by Josh A. Cagan, Kody Keplinger (book); Directed by Ari Sandel

An Education (2009) Written by Nick Hornby, Lynn Barber (memoir); Directed by Lone Scherfig

Elizabeth (1998) Written by Michael Hirst; Directed by Shekhar Kapur

Erin Brockovich (2000) Written by Susannah Grant; Directed by Steven Soderbergh

Eye in the Sky (2015) Written by Guy Hibbert; Directed by Gavin Hood

Factory Girl (2006) Written by Captain Mauzner; Directed by George Hickenlooper

The Fault In Our Stars (2014) Written by Scott Neustadter, Michael H. Weber, John Green (book); Directed by Josh Boone

The Five-Year Engagement (2012) Written by Jason Segel, Nicholas Stoller; Directed by Nicholas Stoller

Frances Ha (2012) Written by Noah Baumbach, Greta Gerwig; Directed by Noah Baumbach

Frida (2002) Written by Clancy Sigal, Diane Lake, Gregory Nava, Anna Thomas, Hayden Herrera (book); Directed by Julie Taymor

Frost/Nixon (2008) Written by Peter Morgan (and play); Directed by Ron Howard

The Girl on the Train (2016) Written by Erin Cressida Wilson, Paula Hawkins (book); Directed by Tate Taylor

A Girl Walks Home Alone at Night (2014) Written and Directed by Ana Lily Amirpour

Girlhood (2014) Written and Directed by Céline Sciamma

Gone Girl (2014) Written by Gillian Flynn (and book); Directed by David Fincher

Gone With the Wind (1939) Written by Sidney Howard, Margaret Mitchell (book); Directed by Victor Fleming

Grace of Monaco (2014) Written by Arash Amel; Directed by Olivier Dahan

Hideous Kinky (1998) Written by Billy MacKinnon, Esther Freud (book); Directed by Gillies MacKinnon

The Hunger Games (2012) Written by Gary Ross, Suzanne Collins, Billy Ray, Suzanne Collins (book); Directed by Gary Ross

The Hunger Games: Catching Fire (2013) Written by Simon Beaufoy, Michael deBruyn, Suzanne Collins (book); Directed by Francis Lawrence

The Hunger Games: Mockingjay — Part 1 (2014) Written by Peter Craig, Danny Strong, Suzanne Collins (book); Directed by Francis Lawrence

The Hunger Games: Mockingjay — Part 2 (2015) Written by Peter Craig, Danny Strong, Suzanne Collins (book); Directed by Francis Lawrence

The Huntsman: Winter's War (2016) Witten by Evan Spiliotopoulos, Craig Mazin; Directed by Cedric Nicholas-Troyan

Inside Out (2015) Written by Pete Docter, Meg LeFauve, Josh Cooley; Directed by Pete Docter, Ronnie del Carmen

The Invisible Woman (2013) Written by Abi Morgan, Claire Tomalin (book); Directed by Ralph Fiennes

Iris (2001) Written by Richard Eyre, Charles Wood, John Bayley (books); Directed by Richard Eyre

The Iron Lady (2011) Written by Abi Morgan; Directed by Phyllida Lloyd

Joy (2015) Written and Directed by David O. Russell

The Kids Are All Right (2010) Written by Lisa Cholodenko, Stuart Blumberg; Directed by Lisa Cholodenko

La Vie en Rose (2007) Written by Isabelle Sobelman, Olivier Dahan; Directed by Olivier Dahan

The Lady (2011) Written by Rebecca Frayn; Directed by Luc Besson

Made in Dagenham (2010) Written by William Ivory; Directed by Nigel Cole

Maleficent (2014) Written by Linda Woolverton, Charles Perrault (book); Directed by Robert Stromberg

Mamma Mia! (2008) Written by Catherine Johnson (and musical book); Directed by Phyllida Lloyd

Marie Antoinette (2006) Written and Directed by Sofia Coppola

Monster (2003) Written and Directed by Patti Jenkins

Mrs. Parker and the Vicious Circle (1994) Written by Alan Rudolph, Randy Sue Coburn; Directed by Alan Rudolph

Mustang (2015) Written by Deniz Gamze Ergüven, Alice Winocour; Directed by Deniz Gamze Ergüven

My Week With Marilyn (2011) Written by Adrian Hodges, Colin Clark (book); Directed by Simon Curtis

The Other Woman (2015) Written by Melissa Stack; Directed by Nick Cassavetes

Phoenix (2014) Written by Christian Petzold, Harun Farocki, Hubert Monteilhet (book); Directed by Christian Petzold

Philomena (2013) Written by Steve Coogan, Jeff Cope, Martin Sixsmith (book); Directed by Stephen Frears

Precious (2009) Written by Geoffrey Fletcher, Sapphire (book); Directed by Lee Daniels

Pride (2014) Written by Stephen Beresford; Directed by Matthew Warchus

Psycho (1960) Written by Joseph Stefano, Robert Bloch (book); Directed by Alfred Hitchcock

The Revenant (2015) Written by Mark L. Smith, Alejandro G. Iñárritu, Michael Punke (book, partly based on); Directed by Alejandro G. Iñárritu

Ricki and the Flash (2015) Written by Diablo Cody; Directed by Jonathan Demme

Room (2015) Written by Emma Donoghue (and book); Directed by Lenny Abrahamson

Saving Mr. Banks (2013) Written by Kelly Marcel, Sue Smith; Directed by John Lee Hancock

Spotlight (2015) Written by Tom Singer, Josh McCarthy; Directed by Josh McCarthy

Spy (2015) Written and Directed by Paul Feig

Star Wars Episode VII: The Force Awakens (2015) Written by Lawrence Kasdan, J.J. Abrams, Michael Arndt; Directed by J.J. Abrams

Suffragette (2015) Written by Abi Morgan; Directed by Sarah Gavron

Trainwreck (2015) Written by Amy Schumer; Directed by Judd Apatow

Wadjda (2012) Written and Directed by Haifaa Al-Mansour

We Bought a Zoo (2011) Written by Aline Brosh McKenna, Cameron Crowe, Benjamin Mee (book); Directed by Cameron Crowe

What to Expect When You're Expecting (2012) Written by Shauna Cross, Heather Hach, Heidi Murkoff (book); Directed by Kirk Jones

Wild (2014) Written by Nick Hornby, Cheryl Strayed (book); Directed by Jean-Marc Vallée

About the Author

Helen Jacey, Ph.D., is a screenwriter, story consultant, international speaker, and author. Her advanced screenwriting seminar *Helen Jacey's Writing the Heroine's Story* has been hosted in numerous countries since 2010. Helen also teaches at Bournemouth University. She is author of the forthcoming *Elvira Slate Investigations* series of crime novels.

For more information, visit www.helenjacey.com.

{ THE MYTH OF MWP }

In a dark time, a light bringer came along, leading the curious and the frustrated to clarity and empowerment. It took the well-guarded secrets out of the hands of the few and made them available to all. It spread a spirit of openness and creative freedom, and built a storehouse of knowledge dedicated to the betterment of the arts.

The essence of the Michael Wiese Productions (MWP) is empowering people who have the burning desire to express themselves creatively. We help them realize their dreams by putting the tools in their hands. We demystify the sometimes secretive worlds of screenwriting, directing, acting, producing, film financing, and other media crafts.

By doing so, we hope to bring forth a realization of 'conscious media' which we define as being positively charged, emphasizing hope and affirming positive values like trust, cooperation, self-empowerment, freedom, and love. Grounded in the deep roots of myth, it aims to be healing both for those who make the art and those who encounter it. It hopes to be transformative for people, opening doors to new possibilities and pulling back veils to reveal hidden worlds.

MWP has built a storehouse of knowledge unequaled in the world, for no other publisher has so many titles on the media arts. Please visit www.mwp.com where you will find many free resources and a 25% discount on our books. Sign up and become part of the wider creative community!

Onward and upward,

Michael Wiese
Publisher/Filmmaker